®

SALT LAKE 2002™

WHITE GOLD

The U.S. Olympic Team at the XIX Olympic Winter Games

Publisher
Wallace Sears

Editor
Darcy Steinfeld

Photo Editor
Teri Hayt

Book Designer
Keith Dunn

Associate Editor
Keri Kahn

Coordinators
Fran Henderson   **Brad Sinclair**

Editorial Assistant
Trey Mcclure

Photography
Allsport Photography / London, New York, Los Angeles, Sydney, Melbourne
AP/WideWorld Photos   **Long Photography**
Gary Bogden/Orlando Sentinel   **Gina Ferazzi/**L.A. Times
Chris Lee/St. Louis Post   **Reuters**
Anacleto Rapping/L.A. Times   **David Sanders/**Arizona Daily Star

Special Imaging Assistance Provided by
Jon Hayt

Special Editorial Assistance Provided by
The U.S. Olympic Committee

Managing Director for Media & Public Relations
Mike Moran

Director of Media Services
Bob Condron

Director of Marketing
Mike Wilson

Special thanks to
**U.S. Biathlon Association   The U.S. Bobsled & Skeleton Federation
USA Curling   The U.S. Figure Skating Association
USA Hockey   The U.S. Luge Association
The U.S. Ski and Snowboard Association   U.S. Speedskating**

Pachyderm Press

SANDY BALDWIN
PRESIDENT, U.S. OLYMPIC COMMITTEE

The XIX Olympic Winter Games in Salt Lake City may have been our finest hour. We took a competitive leap that no team in Olympic history has matched.

We almost tripled our previous best medal total in the Olympic Winter Games, and we accomplished these amazing goals through the most diversified winter team in history.

There were so many firsts for these outstanding Americans:

- Most medals ever for a United States Team.
- First African-American gold medal winner.
- First African-American male medal winners.
- First Mexican-American gold medal winner.
- First Cuban-American medal winner.
- First Native-American Winter Olympic athlete.
- Five medals by Asian-American athletes.
- Second to Germany among all countries in total medals.
- One medal short of tying for the overall country lead.
- A drug-free Games for the U.S. Team.
- Being part of the best Winter Games in history.

Our athletes were outstanding, in competition as well as setting role models for generations of youngsters throughout the country. Somewhere there is a young Hispanic who wants to be a speedskater like Derek Parra or Jennifer Rodriguez. There is a young African-American girl who wants to be a bobsledder like Vonetta Flowers. There is a Native-American youngster who wants to be a figure skater like Naomi Lang.

The U.S. Team set a standard that's going to be hard to match, and they did it with class and honor. The U.S. Olympic Committee is proud of these 209 athletes, and we are proud that we were able to fund, to equip, to help train, to outfit, and to provide travel in partnership with our outstanding National Governing Bodies and our sponsors.

We'd also like to congratulate Mitt Romney and the Salt Lake Olympic Organizing Committee for its dedication to excellence in hosting these Games. The venues were excellent, the athletes and fans were treated royally, and every face you encountered in the cities and on the mountains came with a smile. For us, these Games may never be matched.

The 2002 Olympic Winter Games were magic for America. With the memories still fresh from Sept. 11, it was a small step to help this country heal its wounds. It was a moment when America could be proud of its Olympians and its Olympic Games.

(L-R) Jack Shea, Jim Jr., and Jim Sr. shortly after Jim Jr. qualified for the 2002 U.S. Olympic Skeleton Team at Mt. Van Hoevenberg in Lake Placid, New York. Jack Shea was killed in an automobile accident in January, just a few weeks before Jim Jr. won the gold medal.

BREAKFAST WITH THE OLYMPIANS

February 17, 2002

The following text is from a speech Jim Shea Sr. gave to those attending the XEROX Breakfast With The Olympians on Feb. 17, 2002 in Salt Lake City, Utah. The United States Olympic Committee awarded its highest honor, the Olympic Torch Award, to Jim Shea Sr., to honor his late father, the patriarch of the Shea family that has produced three generations of U.S. Olympic athletes.

"Upon the death of Jack Shea (my Dad) I noticed on his desk a sheet of yellow legal paper with his prepared comments to those attending the breakfast.

'I sincerely thank XEROX and XEROX guests, together with the United States Olympic Committee, for this gathering to honor the United States Olympians and me as an Olympian.

For 70 years as an Olympian, I have proudly proclaimed the value of the Olympic ideal in 'promulgating peace through friendly competition.' I implore all U.S. Olympians to do the same. By doing so, you honor your country and bring glory to sports.'

Those were Dad's words.

I would add that the entire country is so proud of each and every one of you. I hope you feel the pride and make these Games an event your memory will carry with you forever. I know you will never forget that feeling you had when you walked into the Opening Ceremony. For me, it was 1964, and to be honest, it feels like it was only yesterday.

As Olympians you will be held to a higher standard for your entire life. Please don't back away from this challenge. You have all worked so hard for this special and unique recognition.

Keep the flame burning.

God bless each and every one of you.

Thank you."
Jim Shea Sr.

Todd Warshaw/Pool/Getty Images

TABLE OF CONTENTS

U.S. Olympic Committee
One Olympic Plaza, Colorado Springs, CO 80909-5760   719/632-5551

Published under license from the U.S. Olympic Committee by:
Pachyderm Press, P.O. Box 661016, Birmingham, AL 35266-1016
Telephone 205/822-4139   Fax 205/979-7906   www.pachydermpress.com

ISBN 0-9639505-9-2

OLYMPIC WINTER GAMES SA

XIX OLYMPIC WINTER GAMES

President George W. Bush poses with members of the U.S. Team during the Opening Ceremony.

AP Photo/Jerry Lampen/Pool

Facing page: Fireworks burst over Rice-Eccles Olympic Stadium and the Olympic Cauldron during the Opening Ceremony.

usa
2002
XIX OLYMPIC WINTER GAMES

by Mike Eruzione
Captain of the Gold Medal 1980 USA Hockey Team
"THE MIRACLE ON ICE"

What was my greatest thrill as an Olympic athlete? People have asked me that many times over the years. After February 8, 2002 my answer has changed.

In the past, some people have been surprised by my answer. When my teammates and I won the gold medal in 1980, it was an unbelievable experience, and the feeling I had -- we all had -- sharing the platform together was something that is almost beyond words to describe.

But to me, the Opening Ceremony is probably the most special part of the Olympic Games. I still believe that marching in the Opening Ceremony was my greatest thrill, because if you don't get there, then none of the other things afterward will ever happen. So I look at the Opening Ceremony as the starting point. All of the time and work and effort you put in through all those years -- it's when you

Captain Mike Eruzione and other members of the 1980 gold medal-winning USA Men's Hockey Team hold up the torch before lighting the Olympic Cauldron at the Opening Ceremony.

Previous page: Native American performers enter Rice-Eccles Olympic Stadium during the Opening Ceremony.

march in, that you realize you've "made it!" After that, everything that happens is icing on the cake.

Now, I look at lighting the Olympic Cauldron at the Opening Ceremony in Salt Lake City as the ultimate honor for an Olympic athlete -- along with my teammates. Who would have ever believed it could happen to me? To us?

I guess the older you get the more reflective you get on your life. When I was standing up there with my teammates, holding the torch, and looking down at all those great athletes and all those people, the first thing that crossed my mind was how many other people had been involved in carrying that flame. I thought about how it started in Athens, Greece, arrived in Atlanta, and then it went all across our country. The flame was carried by thousands of men and women . . . young girls and boys . . . people with disabilities . . . great athletes . . . great inspirational stories, and then here we were. And I was holding

it on the last journey.

It was a great feeling of pride knowing that the Salt Lake Organizing Committee thought enough of our 1980 USA Hockey Team to give us this honor. Again, I recalled marching in the Opening Ceremony in Lake Placid, and if that had never happened, obviously I would never have had the opportunity to light the cauldron in Salt Lake City.

Life goes in phases. You march in the Opening Ceremony in 1980. You compete as an Olympic athlete for two weeks. You have the distinction of receiving a gold medal. And then, you think it's over.

Now 22 years later, to be in Salt Lake City, the first time the Winter Olympics has been back in the U.S. since, and for our 1980 Hockey Team to be the people who kick off the games -- it made everything come full-circle. It was an incredible honor!

Gary M. Prior/Getty Images

AP Photo/Lionel Cironneau

Top left: Johann Muehlegg, the Spanish skier who dominated the cross country events at the 2002 Olympic Winter Games, was stripped of one of his three gold medals after testing positive for a performance-enhancing drug.

Top right: A couple of skating fans hold up signs protesting the outcome of the figure skating pairs competition.

Bottom left: Jamie Sale of Canada shrugs off her disappointment alongside her partner, David Pelletier, after the pairs free program figure skating event.

Bottom right: David Pelletier and Jamie Sale of Canada stand with Anton Sikharulidze and Elena Berezhnaya of Russia on the podium with their double gold medals in the pairs.

Robert Laberge/Getty Images

Clive Brunskill/Getty Images

Shaun Botterill/Getty Images

Steven Page, the lead singer of The Barenaked Ladies, dressed in a Canadian speedskating uniform for their performance at the Olympic Medals Plaza.

And, it was a moment that I wish could have lasted longer. We all had such a feeling of pride. My heart was pumping like you can't believe as I held the torch, and the sound in Rice-Eccles Stadium was amazing. I remember pointing up to the sky to my Mother, because I know she would have been very proud of me. I stood there thinking that this was the ultimate honor for all of us. I just couldn't believe it.

Of course, this had been a pretty big secret. The team and I did not know exactly what we were doing during the Opening Ceremony, but everybody had been asking us about it. Now, I had known for six months that I was going to be involved, but I didn't know how. Mitt Romney had asked me to participate, but said he didn't know what my role would be. Then, one week before the Games, the whole team was contacted and told to come in early. But still, no one said anything about what we would do.

Finally, at one o'clock in the morning Thursday, we were told that we were going to light the cauldron on Friday night. We had about 16 hours to keep it quiet --

John Gichigi/Getty Images

Harry How/Getty Images

Fans gather to hear the music of the Dave Matthews Band at Olympic Medals Plaza.

Facing Page: The Salt Lake Temple with a back drop of a figure skating banner on a building during the Salt Lake City Olympic Winter Games.

were. They got to celebrate with the athletes in their victory, and it gave them some fun at the same time. It made the Olympic Winter Games special for everyone.

Every Olympic Games has a controversy of some sorts, and Salt Lake did, too. As for the pairs skating situation -- historically, whether it's the Olympics or World Championships, there have always been disagreements. Anytime you have judges making decisions . . . well, what I might see one way another judge may see another way.

I thought that the International Olympic Committee (IOC) and the International Skating Union (ISU) did a great job of addressing it right away so that it didn't drag on and take away from other events, athletes and competitions.

Having an Olympic Games without a controversy is like . . . well . . . having a hockey game without a player going into the penalty box!

One other negative that I saw was the doping cases. I've been around the Olympic community a long time now, and year in and year out I've seen how the IOC continues to clean up competition. There are considerably fewer athletes using illegal supplements today than years ago. I know! The IOC and the various National Olympic Committees are doing a much better job of testing the athletes and finding out who's on what. It's unfortunate. To me I can't believe that true competitors would want to cheat, but then, everybody wants to get an "edge". If that's the way some individuals do it, they should realize that eventually they're going to get caught and pay the price. History tells you that there will be some drug problems with some athletes. You just address the issue and you move on. It still is only a small part of what became a great Olympic Games.

And I've always found that for every negative in life you have a positive. Like the USA berets! They were great! Wouldn't you like to be the guy from Roots that dreamed them up? I brought some home for my family. Just like scores and scores of other people did. Hey, it's the Olympic Games. It's a fad. Every Olympic Games seems to have some kind of trademark. Years ago they wanted those nice Norwegian sweaters when I was in Lillehammer. For Salt Lake, it was the berets.

During the whole time I was in Salt Lake there was one individual that I never got a chance to meet, and I wish I had -- IOC President Jacques Rogge. Having an athlete as the president of the entire Olympic Movement is wonderful, in my opinion. It tells you a lot about the quality of athletes we've had over the years; that one of us can rise to the top level. It

President Jacques Rogge presents Dr. Bengt Saltin of Sweden with the IOC Olympic Prize on Sport Sciences endowed by Pfizer in a special ceremony at the Athlete Village.

Yang Yang (A) (right) won the gold medal in the women's 1000m short track speedskating final. It was the very first Olympic Winter Games gold medal for China.

Al Bello/Getty Images

Danielle Goyette #15 waves her Canadian flag after winning the women's ice hockey gold medal game.

Robert Laberge/Getty Images

Alisa Camplin of Australia receives the gold medal for the women's freestyle aerials. Australia celebrated Camplin's achievement by creating a postage stamp in her honor.

Leonhard Foeger/Reuters

Male members of the Croatian Olympic team kneel around their teammate, gold medalist Janica Kostelic, as she celebrates winning the women's giant slalom competition. Kostelic became the first Alpine skier ever to win four medals at one Olympic Winter Games when she won the gold with a total time of 2 minutes 30.01 seconds. Kostelic had already won two golds and one silver medal earlier in the Games.

AP Photo/Seiko Timing

Norway's Thomas Alsgaard, bottom, thrusts his ski forward to tie with his teammate Frode Estil for the silver medal in the men's cross country pursuit.

Gold medalist Jim Shea (far right) poses with his mother, Judy, (left) and Prince Albert of Monaco after he won the men's skeleton final.

AP Photo/Charlie Booker

Children cheer on the Olympic Torchbearers during the 2002 Salt Lake Olympic Torch Relay in Berthoud, Colorado.

adds a lot of credibility to the whole Olympic Movement.

I also admire his decision to stay in the Olympic Village with the athletes. In Salt Lake, the athletes had a real hands-on approach with him. Here's someone who is going to be making decisions on many more Olympic Games, and for him to be in the Village, talking with the competitors, gives inside information and input that I think is invaluable.

There were a lot of tremendous things that happened at the Salt Lake Olympics. When you look at the accomplishments of the Australian and Chinese teams winning their first gold medals ever at a Winter Olympics, it shows you how far the Winter Games reach, and how important they have become. We're going to see more medals from Australia and China in the future. Why? Because the athletes' performances were well reported back in their countries. I can promise you that there were some young kids who were watching in Sydney, Melbourne, Beijing and Canton who have already said "I'd like to try that sport." You'll see this continue...and with other countries, as well!

Of course, Team USA didn't do badly, either...in fact, it was the best Winter Olympic performance in our country's history. The medal count demonstrates what the U.S. National Governing Bodies and the U.S. Olympic Committee are trying to accomplish, and that level of success was finally reached after years of work. America's athletes are reaping the rewards of the opportunities that have been provided to them. Years ago we didn't have facilities as advanced as they are right now. I think sports enthusiasts in this country are realizing how important the Olympic Games are; Summer and Winter.

These medals come at a cost. And the cost is not only the athletes training themselves, but the support they're getting from their family and friends, corporate America and the U.S. Olympic Committee. Everyone I've listed is working to give these athletes the chance to be the best.

Fireworks light up the sky above the Rice-Eccles Olympic Stadium during the Closing Ceremony.

Facing Page: The largest blacklight display ever is performed on the ice during the Closing Ceremony of the Salt Lake City Olympic Winter Games at the Rice-Eccles Olympic Stadium in Salt Lake City, Utah.

Following Pages: Vonetta Flowers (right) and Jill Bakken tearfully embrace after winning the gold medal in women's bobsleigh.
Casey FitzRandolph (left) and Kip Carpenter proudly wave their American flags after winning gold and bronze respectively in the 500m long track event.

I also think much of the credit should go to our USOC organization, especially President Sandy Baldwin and CEO Lloyd Ward. Our Olympic Committee set a goal with these Olympic Winter Games. The target was 20 medals, and they won a few more. Our total was 34, to be exact; the largest number ever. Some people say that this was a result of all the money that was spent. However, it's not just the facilities, or the money. The athletes themselves must want to train. And I think these athletes, because of their performance, and the success they've had, indicates that the dedication is there with our youth, which will go hand-in-hand with the commitment of the U.S. Olympic Committee.

Tradition plays a big part in the Olympic Games, too. Tradition carried on by many of the athletes, such as Jimmy Shea. When he won the gold medal in skeleton, it was as a third generation U.S. Olympic athlete. We've had more than a century of Olympic Games competition, and now many athletes carry on the tradition established by their family, just like Jim did. There is obviously a passion in his family that Jim recognized and wanted to be a part of. It says a lot for him, his father, and his grandfather.

Salt Lake's Closing Ceremony was as good as the Opening Ceremony. My wife said that Harry Connick, Jr. singing "Over the Rainbow" with Dorothy Hamill skating was just an absolute perfect way to end the Games. What better person to skate to that song than her.

And what better way to end this wonderful celebration of sport and performances by athletes from all over the world.

It was amazing to me how far things have come in 22 years. We had 10,000 people in the stands in Lake Placid. There were 60,000 people in the stands in Salt Lake City.

One thing has stayed the same, though: the excitement that was generated from the Opening Ceremony carried on throughout the Games to the Closing Ceremony. It was something that I'll always remember.

But then, there are many things about the Salt Lake City Winter Olympic Games that I'll never forget. One is the people. The smiles on just about everybody's face every day. Wherever you were, wherever you went, whatever street you were on, you were greeted by smiles. Whether you were trading pins, trying to buy a beret, or waiting in line to go to an event; it was all positive. It was a happy, "good feeling" Olympic Games.

From an American standpoint, the success of our own athletes made it that much more enjoyable. But when we saw the athletes from all over the world compete at the top of their form in such a wonderful place, you knew they were having a good time, and that they enjoyed the Games as competitors as much as we did as spectators. That was something that I have not always recognized in other Olympic cities.

This, to me, was the perfect Olympic Winter Games.

BIATHLON

By Jerry Kokesh,
U.S. Biathlon Association

The 2002 Olympic biathlon competitions at Soldier Hollow will be remembered for three things: spectacular conditions, record-breaking performances, and Norwegian Ole Einar Bjoerndalen.

The U.S. team recorded some of their best placements in Winter Olympic history, leaving Soldier Hollow excited about their accomplishments and with a renewed vigor for the future.

The biathlon competition kicked off with the women's 15km individual event. The U.S. women saw their best finish in the individual competition when Rachel Steer, a veteran at 24, claimed the 31st position. The Alaskan missed only two shots, but lacked the ski speed to improve her standing. Kristina Sabasteanski from Standish, Maine finished a disappointing 55th and teammate Kara Salmela finished 59th. Though the results were not what the U.S. team had hoped for, they were an improvement over the Nagano Olympic Winter Games and an encouraging step toward the future.

Kristina Sabasteanski from Standish, Maine rests while she awaits her score in the women's 15km individual biathlon event.

Mike Hewitt/Getty Images

The U.S. men also had something to cheer about on the first day of competition. Jeremy Teela scored a record-tying 14th place for Team USA in the 20km individual. This was the fifth time in history that a U.S. Olympic biathlete had finished 14th, but it was the first time in 30 years that it had occurred. Teela's two penalties were a personal best in the individual competition. Teammate Jay Hakkinen missed one more target and followed in 26th position. Two American athletes in the top-30 marked the beginning of a record-topping week for the U.S. biathletes.

In the sprint competitions, Teela finished 20th, while Hakkinen once again finished 26th. Salmela and local favorite Andrea Nahrgang finished 49th and 50th, respectively.

Of all the stars in biathlon, Norwegian Ole Einar Bjoerndalen shone the brightest at the 2002 Olympic Games. He swept the men's individual events, winning gold in the 20km individual, 10km sprint, and the 12.5km pursuit. Bjoerndalen completed his set of four gold medals by anchoring the winning Norwegian men's 4 x 7.5km relay.

Much like Bjoerndalen, the German women were the best in the Soldier Hollow stadium. Kati Wilhelm, the 2001 World Champion in the sprint, proved unbeatable. She was perfect in the shooting range and as a former international competitor in cross country, dominant on the ski tracks. Wilhelm's countrywoman, Uschi Disl, claimed the silver by missing only one target. Magdalena Forsberg from Sweden took home the bronze, beating her old rival from Norway, Liv Grete Poiree, by a mere 3.7 seconds.

The inaugural pursuit competitions proved to be the

Anchorage, Alaska's Rachel Steer on her way to a team-best 31st place finish in the women's 15km individual biathlon event.

Andrea Nahrgang of Wayzata, Minnesota glides across the snow in the women's 7.5km sprint.

most exciting events on the Olympic biathlon schedule. With a short course and the top 60 from the sprint separated by a little over three minutes at the start, the pursuits are fast and furious. Mistakes on the shooting range are costly and an athlete can move up or down with just one bad shooting round.

Hakkinen skied a great race. The 1997 World Junior Biathlon Champion left the stadium in eighth position, missing only one of 20 shots. Leading a pack of 10, Hakkinen had expended all of his energy and finished 13th. This was his lucky 13, as it broke the record for a finish by a U.S. biathlete in the Olympic Winter Games. In 42 years of Olympic biathlon, no American had ever finished higher.

Overcome with emotion at his achievement, Hakkinen had broken the "14th place curse." Teammate Teela slipped slightly from his 20th start position to 23rd at the finish. The Alaskan duo gave the U.S. its best composite results ever in Olympic biathlon competition, and dreams of medals in the next Olympic Winter Games.

With machine-like precision, Bjoerndalen once again dominated the field in the pursuit. He led from start to finish, recording a single penalty in the first and last shooting stages. These he quickly out-skied to claim his third gold medal. France's Raphael Poiree, husband of Liv Grete Poiree, claimed the silver, and Rico Gross of Germany went home with the bronze.

The women's pursuit gave the struggling Russian team its first gold medal. Olga Pyleva, fourth in the individual, missed only one target to claim the title. German Kati Wilhelm desperately wanted a second gold, but had to settle for silver. Wilhelm's four missed shots were more than even the speed queen could outrun, though she gave it her all. She missed the top spot by a mere 5.3 seconds. In the race of her life, Irina Nikoultchina of Bulgaria recorded two penalties to claim bronze by 2.5 seconds over Liv Grete Poiree. Poiree, like Wilhelm, missed four shots, dooming her medal hopes.

After the excitement of the pursuits, the women's and men's 4 x 7.5km relays were little more than assertions of dominance by Norway and Germany. The German women placed three medalists on their squad, while the indomitable Bjoerndalen anchored the Norwegian men's team. Germany breezed to an easy win in the women's event, recording just a single penalty. The Norwegian women followed, almost a full minute ahead of their closest competitors. In the men's event, "King Bjoerndalen" led the Norwegians to his fourth gold, a feat never before seen in Olympic biathlon competition. The Germans grabbed the silver in a close battle with the French.

Clive Brunskill/Getty Images

Mike Hewitt/Getty Images

Jeremy Teela from Anchorage, Alaska finished 23rd in the men's 12.5km sprint event at Soldier Hollow.

Alaskan Jay Hakkinen broke the U.S. record for a finish in the 12.5km pursuit event.

Mike Hewitt/Getty Images

A biathlete shoots in the prone position under the watchful eye of the crowd. An impressive amount of the Soldier Hollow course was visible from the stands.

Competitors during the prone shooting section of the men's 4 x 7.5km biathlon relay at Soldier Hollow in Heber City.

Florence, Vermont's Lawton Redman during a skiing portion of the men's 10km sprint event.

Dan Campbell of Hastings, Minn. and Lawton Redman of Florence, Vt. ran the final two relay legs for the U.S. men. The two Olympic rookies both needed four extra rounds in the shooting range and the extra rounds, plus a penalty, dropped the U.S. team from a high position of 12th to 15th at the end. This result is still two spots better than Nagano four years ago. Hakkinen characterized the performance of the U.S. relay team after the competition.

"We really have not focused on the relay for over two years, so this competition was simply a culmination of the Games for us," Hakkinen said. "We have had a great Olympic Games with some of our best results ever. Our team is looking forward to doing well in upcoming World Cups. I had the third best time in the pursuit and I consider that my paper medal! But seriously, the crowds really inspired our performances and we hope that they will continue to follow our sport as we prepare for Torino."

These Olympic Winter Games biathlon competitions have set the tone for the future. They crowned a "King" in Bjoerndalen, and saw the "Royal Family" of the German women dominate. More importantly to biathlon, these Games exposed the sport's many stars -- who combine mental and physical strength -- to a growing audience in the U.S. and around the world. From what was witnessed at Soldier Hollow during these 10 days in February, biathlon could soon become the king of the Olympic Nordic sports. usa 2002

A group of skiers take a turn in the men's 4 x 7km biathlon relay. The U.S. team finished in 15th place, two spots better than their Nagano finish.

BOBSLEIGH & SKELETON

Driver Brian Shimer and Mike Kohn (front) of the USA II team alongside USA I teammates Bill Schuffenhauer and Garrett Hines cheer as they watch the Swiss team fail to take a medal placing. This meant that both American four-man teams would win Olympic medals, the first time in 46 years for The U.S. Team.

BOBSLEIGH

By Julie Urbansky, U.S. Bobsled and Skeleton Federation

The sport of bobsleigh has been a part of the Olympic Winter Games since 1924 in France. A push to get women's bobsleigh on the Olympic ticket began in the mid-1990s and was finally granted in October of 1999. Utah Olympic Park was the site of the 2002 bobsleigh competitions, and the air was filled with the roar of sleds, the waving of flags, and the sound of cowbells.

The U.S. men's bobsleigh team came into the 2002 Olympic Winter Games having not won an Olympic medal since 1956. Carrying a 46-year medal drought on their shoulders, they were determined to prove that 2002 was the year it would end.

Texan Todd Hays came close in the two-man competition. Hays and two-time Olympian Garrett Hines sat in fifth place after heats one and two, 0.36 seconds off the gold medal. In the second day of two-man, Hays and Hines rallied, putting pressure on Switzerland's Martin Annen and Beat Hefti, but fell short of a medal. The duo moved up one place, into fourth, and missed a bronze medal by 0.03 seconds. Their combined time was 3:10.65.

Jamie Squire/Getty Images

Silver medalists Todd Hays, Randy Jones, Bill Schuffenhauer and Garrett Hines know they have a good time as they cross the finish line in the four-man event.

Jamie Squire/Getty Images

The USA II sled of Brian Shimer, Mike Kohn, Doug Sharp and Dan Steele speed past the crowd at Utah Olympic Park on their way to a bronze medal.

Robert Laberge/ Getty Images

The USA I team of Todd Hays and Garrett Hines crosses the finish line in the two-man event. They missed a bronze medal by 0.03 seconds.

"I am proud of the way that we came back," Hays said. "But we were still a little bit short. But I have to deal with it and shake it off and come back for the four-man."

Their fourth place finish is the second highest finish in the two-man bobsleigh for the U.S. since 1952. Naples, Fla. native and five-time Olympian Brian Shimer combined with 1998 veteran Darrin Steele to finish in ninth place in 3:11.93.

"It was sad that it was my last two-man race ever . . . but the joy is being here in the U.S. and representing my country," Shimer said.

German driver Christoph Langen, a three-time Olympic medalist and eight-time world champion, and Markus Zimmerman slid to gold with a combined time of 3:10.11. Langen and Christian Reich of

Switzerland were tied following heats one and two, but Reich faltered, giving Langen the win. Annen and Hefti took the bronze in 3:10.62.

In the four-man event, Hays was determined to quench the medal drought.

"Historically, I do better in four-man than in two-man," Hays said. "So if we can get one more place, I can bring home that elusive Olympic medal that the U.S. has been seeking for 46 years."

Hays and his crew of Bill Schuffenhauer, three-time Olympian Randy Jones, and Hines laid down two tremendous runs and were in the lead after day one. Annen and Germany's Andre Lange were tied for second.

Shimer and his crew of Mike Kohn, Doug Sharp, and Dan Steele sat in fifth place after day one.

Team USA II, driven by Brian Shimer, pushes off in the four-man event. Five-time Olympian Shimer completed his career with a bronze medal in this event.

Shaun Botterill/Getty Images

The USA I sled, with American bald eagles painted on the sides, streaks past the fans on the way to a silver medal.

"Todd's runs were great," said U.S. men's bobsleigh Assistant Coach Greg Sand. "We are just going to come out and stick to the game plan and try to have fast starts and down times. If we do that, we should end up on the podium."

Little did Sand know that was exactly what was going to happen.

Chants of "USA" filled Utah Olympic Park as Hays' team took the hill. With a run of 47.22, Hays' crew dropped to third place in the standings. Shimer's team rallied and moved up to fourth to start the last heat of his career.

As the final sleds descended from the start at Utah Olympic Park, both Shimer and Hays knew that they had to lay down great runs to earn a spot on the podium. Shimer drove down the fastest heat of the day and finished with a combined time of 3:07.86. Hays was next down and beat Shimer with a combined time of 3:07.81, but the drama was still unfolding.

In an amazing turn of events, Switzerland's Annen faltered in the fourth heat and continued to lose speed down the track. The bronze medalist in two-man, Annen and his crew of Silvio Schaufelberger, Beat Hefti and Cedric Grand dropped to fourth place and secured two medals for the U.S. men. The drought was over.

With Langen pulling out of four-man due to injury, Lange carried his nation's medal hopes on his shoulders. He would not disappoint, and his crew of Enrico Kuehn, Kevin Kuske and Carsten Embach took home the

gold in 3:07.51. Hays finished in second and Shimer took the bronze.

"In my last Olympic Games, my last race, my last run, I was still not sure that I was going to be winning a medal," Shimer said. "To be able to stand in the winner's box and watch the sleds come down behind me, and beat them out for the bronze. This is a fairy tale ending."

Todd Hays was ecstatic following the event. "It is such an honor to represent this country. To come away with a medal is amazing. We knew the Germans would be tough. We're really happy with silver. I'm proud to be a member of this team. What an honor."

Garrett Hines and Randy Jones became the second and third African-Americans to win medals at the Olympic Winter Games, following in the steps of fellow bobsledder Vonetta Flowers (see below).

Following his tremendous performance, Shimer was honored by his fellow U.S. athletes by being chosen to carry the U.S. flag into the Closing Ceremony of the 2002 Olympic Winter Games.

For the debut of women's bobsleigh, history was in the making for these athletes who fought long and hard to be granted Olympic status. All eyes would fall on these very determined women and their debut in Salt Lake City.

Americans Jean Racine and Gea Johnson were the favorites going into the inaugural event, along with German drivers Susi Erdmann and Sandra Prokoff. Switzerland's Francoise Burdet is always a medal threat.

Jill Bakken and Vonetta Flowers celebrate a gold medal-winning run in the inaugural women's bobsleigh event.

Mike Hewitt/Getty Images

Jamie Squire/Getty Images

Todd Hays and Garrett Hines barely missed a bronze medal in the men's two-man bobsleigh event.

Waterford, Mich. native Racine, a two-time World Cup champion, combined with Johnson in December of 2001 and saw immediate results. They were the heavy favorites, expected to waltz in to an easy victory. But it was not meant to be for the duo. Racine and Johnson faltered at the start, with times of 5.54 and 5.58 seconds. Johnson, ailing from a hamstring injury, slipped at the beginning of the second run. Despite Racine's tremendous driving, USA I finished in fifth place in a two-heat combined time of 1:38.73. Johnson had to be helped off the ice.

"We gave every ounce of ourselves," Racine said.

Known as the underdogs, USA II's Jill Bakken and Vonetta Flowers rose to the occasion. A veteran in bobsleigh since 1994, Bakken teamed with Flowers and were incredible at the push start. In the first heat, the duo broke the start record (5.31) and the track record (48.81) to take the lead.

During the second heat, Prokoff and Ulrike Holzner of Germany would break Bakken and Flowers' start record but would come up short of gold, finishing in second. Their combined time was 1:38.06. Bakken and Flowers won gold in 1:37.76. Erdmann and Nicole Herschmann took the bronze medal in 1:38.29.

Al Bello /Allsport

The men's USA II sled blasts by the beautiful mountain scenery at Utah Olympic Park.

51

The USA I women's sled in action.

Driver Jean Racine and Gea Johnson push off in the women's boblsleigh event.

Gold medalists Jill Bakken and Vonetta Flowers in the USA II sled. A native of Alabama, Flowers is the first African-American athlete ever to win a gold medal at the Olympic Winter Games.

Shaun Botterill/Getty Images

Racine and Johnson slide over the Olympic Rings on their way to a fifth place finish.

Mike Hewitt/Getty Images

Left: Bakken and Flowers begin their celebration after winning gold in the inaugural women's bobsleigh event.

Bakken and Flowers would take the gold and the hearts of fans around the world. With this win, Flowers became the first African-American athlete to win a gold medal in the Olympic Winter Games.

"When I saw it [the scoreboard], my heart dropped," Flowers said. "What can I say? It is a dream come true to win a gold medal for your country."

"It is an amazing feeling," said Bakken following the race. "There was a lot of tough competition, so we definitely had our work cut out for us. The Germans are tough teams to beat."

The spirit of teamwork showed after the race, when Racine ran up to Bakken and hugged her, telling her, "I am very proud of you." And in a true show of Olympic spirit, when the medals were given out, both German teams lifted Bakken and Flowers as they screamed in triumph. Bakken and Flowers were also given the honor of carrying the Olympic Flag into Rice-Eccles Stadium during the Closing Ceremony. usa 2002

53

SKELETON

By Julie Urbansky and LaKesha Whitaker,
U.S. Bobsled and Skeleton Federation

With skeleton making its first reappearance at the Olympic Winter Games since 1948, the focus was on the five Americans who would compete at Utah Olympic Park. Leading up to the games, three out of the six medals ever awarded in skeleton were given to Americans Jennison and John Heaton.

The 2002 team -- featuring an actor, a firefighter, a third-generation Olympian, a computer programmer, and a horticulturist -- trained hard in hopes of adding a few more medals to the tally.

On a snowy day at Utah Olympic Park, the excitement unfolded for the U.S. skeleton team. For third generation Olympian Jim Shea Jr., the fairy tale had a happy ending as he slid to a gold medal in a two-heat combined time of 1:41.96. After losing his grandfather Jack Shea in a fatal automobile accident in late January 2002, Shea followed in his footsteps, giving the Olympic Oath during the Opening Ceremony and then winning the gold medal a few weeks later.

Swiss slider Gregor Stäehli, who won four of the five World Cup races this year, was the first competitor off the hill. He finished with a time of 51.16 seconds.

Austria's Martin Rettl was next, passing Stäehli with a run of 51.02. Duff Gibson of Canada was third in a 51.40. Shea would take the hill next.

Shea had a 50.89 second first run. Snow continued to fall and slow the track for the remaining competitors.

Shea held a 0.13 second lead over Rettl entering the last heat. Trailing the entire way, Shea out drove Rettl in the last turn of the track to take the victory. His two-heat time was 1:41.96, just 0.05 ahead of the colorfully coiffed Rettl.

Stäehli had the best time in the second heat, but it wasn't enough to overtake either Shea or Rettl. Stäehli had a two-heat time of 1:42.15.

Stäehli, a five-time world champion, retired from skeleton in 1994, only to come back in 1999 and rank fifth overall in 2000-2001. He was ranked first in the world coming into the Olympic Games.

USA's Jim Shea takes off on his way to victory in the men's skeleton event. His two-heat time of 1:41.96 was 0.05 ahead of Austrian Martin Rettl.

AP Photo/Douglas C. Pizac

Mike Hewitt/Getty Images

Lea Ann Parsley slides into the finish, winning silver in women's skeleton. The U.S. Team won three of the six medals awarded in 2002 in front of a sellout crowd of 15,000 people.

At the end of his second run, Shea pulled his grandfather's funeral card out of his helmet and rejoiced. His father, 1964 Olympian Jim Shea Sr., and mother Judy were there to greet him.

"It was a great race. My grandpa was with me the whole way," Shea said. "I just tried to concentrate on the basics. There's so much going on. There were 15,000 screaming people. I was just having a blast."

Joining Shea on the podium were close friends Rettl and Stäehli.

"I cannot describe this feeling to be together with Jim Shea on the podium," Rettl said. The 2001 World Champion Rettl finished in 1:42.01.

"It was a great race," Shea said. "More importantly, now that I have a gold medal I can honestly say that the friendships are a lot more important to me than the medals. Being up here with Martin (Rettl) and Gregor (Staehli)...it's unbelievable."

Ireland's Clifton Wrottesley just missed being his country's first Winter Olympic medalist, dropping from his third place finish in the first heat and ending up fourth in 1:42.57. He clocked the highest speeds of the competition, reaching up to 79.3 mph.

Lincoln DeWitt, the 2000-2001 World Cup Champion, bounced back after a poor first run to finish fifth in 1:42.83. Despite his disappointing finish, DeWitt was happy for his fellow teammates.

"I think it's going to be great for the U.S. Team," DeWitt said. "The Olympics is going to be great exposure for skeleton and I think having Americans do well like Jimmy and like the women did, it is really going to do great things for our program."

A disappointing first heat hampered Trumbull, Conn. native Chris Soule, who ranked second in the world this season. He rallied, having a tremendous second heat, but it would prove to be too little. He finished in seventh in 1:42.98.

"I was just going to have the best race I could," Soule said of his goals before the race. "The second run was pretty good for me, I minimized some of the mistakes I made in the first run and I just had to put down a good run and move up some spots."

Soule enjoys working as a stuntman and actor in his spare time, having had parts in GI Jane and Sex and the City.

Matthew Stockman/Getty Images

Chris Soule works as an actor and stuntman when he's not sliding.

In women's action, the U.S. gave the top performances of the day and took the gold and silver over a field of thirteen competitors.

Twenty-one year-old World Cup rookie Tristan Gale, a Salt Lake City native, laid down the fastest time of the first heat in 52.26 seconds, just 0.01 ahead of teammate Lea Ann Parsley (Granville, Ohio) to take the lead in the competition.

Switzerland's Maya Pedersen laid down the fastest time in the second heat, a 52.63, but after a seventh place ranking after run one, would finish with a combined time of 1:45.55. Pedersen, the defending World Champion, finished in fifth place.

Gale, with red, white and blue streaked hair and "USA" painted on her left cheek, won the gold by 0.10 seconds over Parsley. Reigning World Cup Champion Alex Coomber of Great Britain took the bronze.

"Coming across the finish line knowing that I've got a medal was just absolutely amazing," Coomber said.

Gale, the youngest slider on the U.S. team, said her local fan support really helped boost her performance level.

"It was a confidence thing," Gale said of the race.

Donald Miralle/Getty Images

Mike Hewitt/Getty Images

Above: Lincoln Dewitt takes to the ice in the men's skeleton event.

Right: Jim Shea slides past the Olympic Rings at Utah Olympic Park.

Facing page: Jim Shea waves to the crowd while his mother holds the picture of his late grandfather that Jim carried in his helmet on his way to the gold medal.

Clive Brunskill/Getty Images

Gold medalist Tristan Gale slides with determination through the snow.

Below right: Tristan Gale celebrates winning the gold medal in women's skeleton with her teammate Lea Ann Parsley, who won silver.

"I knew that I could slide well here. I just came out and did my best."

Gale had never finished higher than eighth in a World Cup race.

Parsley was very proud of her teammates following the event and pleased with her silver medal.

"I don't care what color (medal) it is," Parsley said. "After watching Jimmy (Shea) win his gold, it just felt good to see our program have such a great day. I was happy for Tristan (Gale), because I know it means so much, not just to us individually, but to USA Skeleton."

Parsley was selected as one of the eight athletes to carry the World Trade Center flag into the Opening Ceremony. Shea and his father, along with Gale, carried the Olympic Flame on its way to the cauldron at the Opening Ceremony.

U.S. Olympic skeleton coach Terry Holland was more than pleased with the team's performance and the way it boosted the public's perception of the sport.

"We've quietly been building the best program in the world and this is our chance to hop out on stage and show everyone how good it was," Holland said. "Hopefully this will be the foundation of a new effort with skeleton to continue to develop and put us on medal stands for years to come."

The U.S. team took three of the six medals in the return of skeleton in front of a sellout crowd of 15,000. In skeleton's Olympic history, the U.S. team has won half of the total medals. Who knows what's in store for the USA skeleton team at Torino in 2006.   usa 2002

Mike Hewitt/Getty Images

Mike Hewitt/Getty Images

All-American girl Tristan Gale waves her flag in triumph. Gale at 21 is the youngest member on the U.S. skeleton team.

Jamie Squire/Getty Images

Mike Schneeberger (middle) releases the stone while sweepers John Gordon (left) and Myles Brundidge guide the stone during the USA vs. France match.

Right: An up-close view of a curling stone as it slides across the ice.

Gary M. Prior/Getty Images

By Rick Patzke, USA Curling

Both the U.S. men's and women's teams competing in curling in the 2002 Olympic Winter Games arrived at The Ice Sheet with plausible medal hopes. Based upon the USA's results in world competition over the past decade, and the experience of the teams in the Olympics, unofficial handicappers viewed the U.S. teams as legitimate contenders in both the men and women's fields.

In the end, the best the U.S. teams could manage was fourth place in the women's field and a tie for seventh in the exceptionally tough men's division. The biggest surprises, however, came elsewhere, as pre-tournament favorites Canada and Sweden failed to capture gold in either competition.

Norway's team edged Canada's rink in the men's gold medal final, claiming a 6-5 victory when Kevin Martin's hammer shot for the win in the 10th end slid an inch too far. Switzerland's Christof Schwaller team won the bronze, denying reigning world champion Peter Lindholm's rink

from Sweden an Olympic medal for the second straight Games.

The U.S. men's team of skip Tim Somerville (Coon Rapids, Minn.), vice skip Mike Schneeberger (Delano, Minn.), second Myles Brundidge (Nekoosa, Wis.), lead John Gordon (Columbia Heights, Minn.) and alternate Don Barcome Jr. (Grand Forks, N.D.), found the drive toward the playoffs to be like a run through wet concrete. After an inspiring 10-5 victory over Sweden's two-time world champions in the first draw of the competition, Somerville's team lost to the powerful Canadian rink and then suffered back-to-back, one-point losses to Germany and Norway. Both of the latter losses came on the last rock of the game, and the effect on the team was more than just a mark in the loss column.

Skip Kari Erickson in action against Great Britain. The U.S. women's team got the nickname of "Kari's Cardiac Kids" because of their come-from-behind finishes in several games.

Team USA, coached by Raymond "Bud" Somerville, got back into the playoff chase by beating Switzerland and France to improve to 3-3, but then lost on the last shot in an extra end for the second time in four games, this time to Denmark. At 3-4, Somerville's team had to win its last two games to position itself for an opportunity to advance to the playoffs. But Finland sealed the Americans' fate in the next draw, handing them a 6-4 loss that once again came down to the final shot of the game. With nothing left to play for but pride, USA returned for the final round robin game against Great Britain. As a final reminder of how strong the riptide was during the week, the Americans suffered yet another last-rock loss, 7-6.

To sum it up, three-time Olympian Somerville said: "Sometimes you just get out-played and out-shot. We played tough, but not good enough. We played our hearts out."

In the women's division, Kelley Law's vaunted team of Canadians was upset in the semifinals by the scrappy Great Britain crew led by Rhona Martin. Just to get to the playoffs, Martin's band had to win tiebreakers over Sweden and Germany. USA's skip, Kari Erickson (Bemidji, Minn.), vice skip Debbie McCormick (Rio, Wis.), second Stacey Liapis (Chicago), lead Ann Swisshelm (Chicago) and alternate Joni Cotten (Mt. Prospect, Ill.) faced Switzerland in the semifinals and suffered their worst defeat of the competition, 9-4 in nine ends. That brought about a medal contest between USA and Canada. This had been a highly anticipated match-up, which both sides had been focusing on
as a showdown for the gold. As it turned out, it was for the bronze, and Canada prevailed, 9-5.

Meanwhile, Great Britain completed its rise from the fringes of the playoffs to the top of the podium, defeating Switzerland on an

Skip Tim Somerville pushes the stone during the men's round robin curling event.

FIGURE SKATING

Michelle Kwan finishes her graceful performance in the ladies' short program at the Salt Lake Ice Center.

Gary M. Prior/Getty Images

Facing page: Sarah Hughes appears to be astounded after her perfectly executed free program. She went on to win the gold medal.

By Bob Dunlop & Laura Fawcett, U.S. Figure Skating Association

Sixteen-year-old Sarah Hughes must have felt like she was dumped right down in the middle of a tornado. One minute, she was just fighting for a spot on the medal podium after finishing fourth in the ladies' short program at the 2002 Olympic Winter Games. The next, she's the shining star of figure skating with an Olympic gold medal around her neck.

Hughes' victory in the ladies' competition was an unexpected finish to the whirlwind of skating competition at the Olympic Winter Games. But while Hughes was crowned as the reigning queen of figure skating, there was also the heartbreak of two other competitors, most notably Michelle Kwan.

Kwan, arguably the favorite in 2002 along with Russian Irina Slutskaya, had the upper hand after the short program. In fact, the U.S. ladies contingent, one of the strongest ever to be sent to an Olympic Winter Games, lived up to its well-deserved reputation,

placing first, third and fourth in the short program.

If there were any lingering demons from 1998, Kwan put them to rest in the Olympic short program, flying across the ice with unmatched grace and a sense of freedom. She cleanly landed her triple Lutz-double toe combination, a double Axel and triple flip in her program to Rachmaninoff's "Piano Concerto No. 3" -- the same program she used at the 1998 Games.

Slutskaya, a three-time world silver medalist, skated with impressive speed and power, landing the more difficult triple Lutz-double loop combination. She won four of the nine first-place marks and was in second behind Kwan.

Sitting in third place after the short program was 2002 U.S. silver medalist Sasha Cohen. The 17-year-old had never even competed in the World Figure Skating Championships, but it didn't seem to matter in the judges' eyes. Cohen skated with lyrical flow and solid consistency, collecting six 5.8s for presentation.

Hughes, meanwhile, hit a triple Lutz-double loop combination, a triple flip and double Axel. Although her presentation marks were as

65

high as 5.7, the judges gave her marks as low as 5.1 for required elements. In fourth place after the short, Hughes focus shifted to just getting on the podium. Because she wasn't in the top three after the short program, her destiny was out of her hands, which eased the pressure for her in the free skate. In order to win gold, Hughes would have to win the free skate, and Kwan would have to finish no higher than third. With the way both Kwan and Slutskaya skated in the short, that seemed like an unlikely probability.

Strange things happen at the Olympics, however.

Hughes was the first of the U.S. ladies to skate in the free skate, and she tore the roof off with one of the most technically ambitious free skates ever done by a woman in Olympic competition. She was simply flawless, landing two triple-triple combinations -- a triple Salchow-triple loop and triple toe-triple loop -- along with three other triples (seven total). She was an athlete at the top of her game.

Cohen had a good skate, but it lacked the technical precision of her short program. She attempted a triple Lutz-triple toe combination, but sat down on the ice on the second jump and later had a wobbly triple Lutz. She landed five other triples in her program to "Carmen," but it wasn't enough to overtake Hughes.

For Kwan, the title was essentially hers to win or lose. Unfortunately, she didn't have her best skate on the one night it meant so much to her. She had trouble on the opening jump of her performance, and later fell on a triple flip, dashing her gold medal hopes.

The competition then rested on Slutskaya's shoulders. She controlled her own destiny in the free skate. A flawless performance would all but seal a first-place finish and a gold medal.

That was not to be, however. She landed five clean triples, but stepped out of a sixth, and did no triple-triple combinations. The program also lacked some of the fire that she

Mike Powell/Getty Images

Al Bello/Getty Images

Top: Seventeen-year-old Sasha Cohen spins during the women's free program. She would finish an impressive fourth in her first Olympic Winter Games.

Bottom: Sarah Hughes breezes across the ice during the ladies' short program, the first part of her gold medal-winning performance in the ladies' individual figure skating event.

Bronze medalist Michelle Kwan performs in the ladies' free program during the Salt Lake City Olympic Winter Games.

T LAKE 2

Ice Hockey

Brian Rolston #12 (back), Doug Weight #39 (left) and Mike York #61 celebrate a 3-2 victory over Russia during the Olympic Winter Games at the E Center in Salt Lake City, Utah.

Harry How/Getty Images

By Yariv Amir, USA Hockey

USA Hockey entered the XIX Olympic Winter Games with high expectations for both its men's and women's ice hockey teams. The women were the defending champions after claiming the sport's first-ever Olympic gold medal in Nagano, Japan, while the men were looking to erase the memory of a disappointing outing in Nagano. To help find some of the magic that spurred Team USA to gold medals on home ice in 1960 and 1980, the U.S.

enlisted the services of 1980 Head Coach Herb Brooks to lead the men's team in Salt Lake City.

The men's tournament arrived with much fanfare as the National Hockey League's best would be skating for gold at the Olympics. However, before the NHLers arrived, two nations would advance from the preliminary round to join the 'Big Six' in the final round. Those two nations were Belarus and Germany. Belarus compiled a 3-0-0 record to join the U.S., Russia and Finland in Pool D, while Germany went 2-1-0 to join the Czech Republic, Canada and Sweden in Pool C.

Brian Bahr/Getty Images

Brian Bahr/Getty Images

Left: American Jeremy Roenick #97 fends off Canadian Scott Niedermayer #27 during the men's ice hockey gold medal game.

Right: Scott Young #48 celebrates his goal over Belarus.

Below: Tony Amonte #11 and Doug Weight #39 pressure goalkeeper Andrei Mezin #31 of Belarus.

Al Bello/Getty Images

Mike York #61 and the rest of Team USA come to congratulate goaltender Mike Richter after defeating Russia 3-2 in the men's ice hockey semifinal.

John LeClair #10 watches as a deflected shot by teammate Brian Rafalski #3 goes between the leg pads of goalie Martin Brodeur #30 of Canada during the second period of the men's ice hockey gold medal game.

The U.S. opened play against Finland on day seven of the Olympic Winter Games. The U.S. and Finland skated to a scoreless first period and the game remained that way until forward Scott Young sent a wrist shot over Finnish goaltender Jani Hurme's shoulder to give the U.S. a 1-0 lead. Team USA would score five more times, including three from forward John LeClair to open play with a 6-0 win. LeClair became the first American since Pat LaFontaine in 1984 to score a hat trick in an Olympic Winter Games.

With the win, the U.S. joined Russia atop the Pool D standings, as the Russians defeated Belarus 6-4 in their opening game. The next day, Russia faced the U.S. in one of the most anticipated games of the tournament, largely due to the two men coaching the teams. U.S. head coach Herb Brooks was also behind the bench during Team USA's "Miracle on Ice" win versus the Soviet Union in 1980, while Russian head coach Slava Fetisov skated that day for the Soviets.

After playing another scoreless first period, the U.S. jumped on top at 6:49 in the second period on a goal by forward Keith Tkachuk. After falling behind, Russia came back to score the next two goals and hold a 2-1 lead with under five minutes to go in the third period. However, the U.S. rallied and forward Brett Hull scored at 15:30 to even up the game at two, where it would finish. Goaltender Mike Richter made 33 stops for the U.S. men. It was the highest-rated ice hockey game on television since Team USA's gold medal game in 1980 versus Finland. The game was watched by more than 20 million viewers.

At 2-0-0 in Pool D, Team USA needed a win against Belarus to assure a first-place finish in the pool. Belarus came out of the gates strong, scoring 20 seconds into the game to take a 1-0 lead. However, the U.S. continued its strong play and overpowered Belarus, scoring the next eight goals to earn an 8-1 win.

The win secured a first-place seed in pool D, and a quarterfinal contest against Germany. The other semifinal games pitted Sweden against Belarus, Canada versus Finland, and Russia versus the Czech Republic.

Day 12 at the Olympic Winter Games saw one of the greatest days

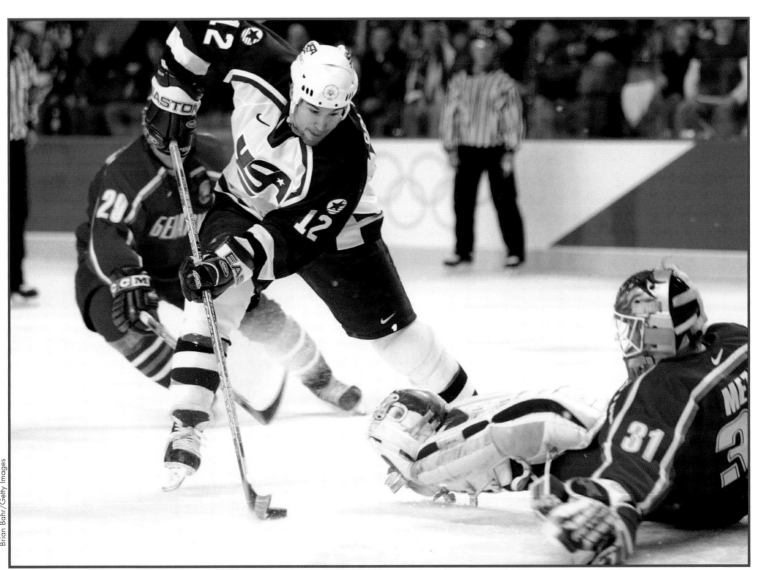

Brian Rolston #12 of the USA pressures goalkeeper Andrei Mezin #31 of Belarus during the Salt Lake City Olympic Winter Games at the E Center.

Following page: Jeremy Roenick is checked on the boards by Germany's Daniel Kunce in the final period of play in a 5-0 victory by the U.S. team.

77

Brian Bahr/Getty Images

Brian Bahr/Getty Images

Brian Bahr/Getty Images

Top left: Laurie Baker #8 of the U.S. Women's Team makes a goal past goaltender Limei Jiang of China in the first period of their preliminary round game.

Top right: Natalie Darwitz and teammates celebrate her goal over Finland.

Left: Tara Mounsey #2 finds herself in a sandwich between Hong Sang #9 and goaltender Limei Jiang #1 of China in the second period of their preliminary round game.

Bottom left: Karyn Bye of the USA passes to one of her teammates during the game against team Germany.

Bottom right: A.J. Mleczko #11 of the USA carries the puck against Canada during the women's ice hockey gold medal game.

Robert Laberge/Getty Images

Brian Bahr/Getty Images

Krissy Wend
preliminary r

Cammi Gran

Goalie Sara DeCosta #1 of the USA makes the save against Cherie Piper #7 of Canada during the women's ice hockey gold medal game.

for hockey in Olympic history, as all four quarterfinals were played. In the first game, Sweden took on Belarus, and in an upset, Belarus defeated Sweden 4-3. The second quarterfinal was equally exciting as Russia earned a 1-0 win over the Czech Republic, knocking the defending gold medalists out of contention.

The next game pitted the U.S. against Germany. Aware of the upsets earlier in the day, the U.S. did not overlook the Germans, defeating them, 5-0, behind a 28-save performance by Mike Richter. Forward Jeremy Roenick scored Team USA's initial first-period goal of the Olympic Games and that proved to be enough to earn the U.S. a semifinal berth. Roenick, John LeClair and Mike Modano each tallied two points in the win for the U.S.

In the fourth quarterfinal of the day, Canada took a 2-0 lead over Finland, and held on to earn a 2-1 win. With four teams advancing, the semifinals were set, as Canada would take on Belarus, while the U.S. and Russia would face each other once again.

With its win over Sweden, Belarus -- the tournament's underdog -- became a fan favorite and received significant support for the semifinal contest with Canada. The Canadians, aware of the threat Belarus could pose, came out hard and Steve Yzerman gave them a 1-0 lead early in the first. However, just minutes later, Belarus knotted the game up at one, making it look like there were still upset possibilities left. However, it only lasted for four minutes, as the Canadians skated to a 7-1 victory and a trip to the gold-medal game.

In the second semifinal, the U.S. faced a familiar foe, Russia, in the second meeting between the two during the Olympic Games. Playing on the 22nd anniversary of the USA-Soviet Union game on Feb. 23, 1980, Team USA looked to have a good start, and Bill Guerin's power-play goal at 15:56 gave the Americans a 1-0 lead. In the second period, defenseman Phil Housley and Scott Young added goals for the U.S. as they continued to dominate the game, out-shooting the Russians 38-11 through two periods. However, the Russians were not done and came out flying in the third period, scoring two goals in 3:10 to make it a 3-2 contest. Mike Richter made 17 third-period saves for the U.S. and staved off a Russian rally, as the Americans advanced to the gold medal game -- their first since winning gold in 1980 at Lake Placid.

"We hope we set a precedent for USA Hockey," Jeremy Roenick said. "We hope we attracted people who were not fans of hockey. I think we made a big stir in the U.S. and I think we've done a lot to encourage hockey in this country."

The bronze medal game featured a rematch of the Russia-Belarus game from the final round. Once again, Belarus hung around, but eventually the Russian offense wore down the Belarussians as they picked up a 7-2 win and the bronze medal.

The gold medal game was hyped to be a showcase for hockey in North America, and the contest itself did not disappoint. The U.S. jumped out to an early 1-0 lead on a goal by Tony Amonte, but it was Canada that left the first period on top, scoring twice in the final five minutes of the

usa
2002

LUGE

Robert Laberge/Getty Image

Mark Grimmette and Brian Martin celebrate silver in the men's doubles luge event.

By Jon Lundin, U. S. Luge Association

In front of a cowbell-clanging pro-U.S. capacity crowd, the American luge team enjoyed its best showing ever in Olympic competition. More than 69,000 fans watched the American team claim two medals in the doubles competition and a combined three top-10 finishes in the men's and women's singles competitions.

In the doubles competition, the U.S. squad matched their accomplishments of four years ago in Nagano, Japan, bagging silver and bronze medals.

"I think that this was the most nervous I've ever been before a race," said Chris Thorpe (Marquette, Mich.), who along with Clay Ives (Lake Placid, N.Y.) won the bronze medal. "To get through the race, and medal, was a very satisfying experience."

Thorpe became just the second slider in Olympic history to win Olympic medals with two different partners. In '98, he raced to a silver medal finish with Gordy Sheer.

Mark Grimmette (Muskegon, Mich.) and Brian Martin

Robert Laberge/Getty Images

Tony Benshoof acknowledges the crowd after his fourth run in the men's luge event.

Robert Laberge/Getty Images

Adam Heidt crosses the finish line to take fourth place and become the highest U.S. male finisher ever in the men's luge event.

(Palo Alto, Calif.), the defending 1998 Olympic bronze medalists, raced to the 2002 Olympic Winter Games' silver medal.

"I was there at eight that morning and saw some friends before the race," Martin said. "They were already rowdy and out of control, and that pumped me up. Having the experience in Nagano helped. I could tune out the crowd when Mark and I raced, but it was great having all my friends there."

Patric Leitner and Alexander Resch won Germany's seventh gold medal in 11 Olympic competitions. Despite almost crashing during their first run, Leitner and Resch's one-day, two-run combined time of 1 minute, 26.082 seconds was .134 seconds faster than Grimmette and Martin, and .138 seconds faster than Thorpe and Ives.

German Georg Hackl's quest to become the first Winter Olympian to win four titles -- in the same discipline -- came up a little short when he fell to Italy's Armin Zoeggeler in the men's singles race, and had to settle for the silver medal. The loss was Hackl's first in Olympic competition since 1988; however, he did become the first winter Olympian to win five medals in the same discipline.

"I feel great, really great to have this awesome career, especially in the Olympic Games," said Hackl, who raced to a two-day, four-run combined time of 2:58.270, just .329 seconds behind Zoeggeler.

Like Hackl, Austria's Markus Prock ended his Olympic career with a medal. The 10-time overall World Cup Champion raced to a bronze medal finish.

"I am happy to have been able to have a fantastic career," said Prock, who is a two-time Olympic silver medalist. "It was always a goal of mine to win a medal at the European Championships, the World Championships and the Olympic Games, which I managed to do. I won a couple of medals and at the same time, I had a great time doing the sport." Prock recorded a four-run total of 2:58.283.

Adam Heidt (Northport, N.Y.) raced to a fourth place finish, the best-ever finish for a U.S. singles slider in Olympic competition.

"Am I disappointed not winning a medal? Absolutely not," said Heidt, who also raced to a ninth place finish in the '98 Winter Games. "To finish behind

85

XIX OLYMPIC WINTER GAMES

Donald Miralle/Getty Images

Above: Chris Thorpe and Clay Ives take a turn during their bronze medal-winning performance in the men's doubles luge event.

Right: A close-up of the determined faces of Mark Grimmette and Brian Martin, silver medalists in the men's doubles luge.

Previous page: Becky Wilczak came in fifth in the women's luge event. Her finish matched the highest ever U.S. finish in the women's luge.

Donald Miralle/Getty Images

Zoeggeler, a three-time Olympic medalist and three-time World Champion, Hackl, a three-time Olympic champion, and Prock, is nothing to be ashamed of." Heidt finished just .323 seconds out of the bronze medal spot.

Teammates Tony Benshoof (White Bear Lake, Minn.) and Nick Sullivan (Oakdale, Minn.), each competing in their first Olympic competition, finished 17th and 26th, respectively.

"I would have liked to record a better result, however, this was a terrific experience," said Benshoof. "The crowd's enthusiasm was overwhelming. Just being a part of everything is something that I'll always cherish."

Germany continued its dominance of the women's singles event. Entering the Games riding a 33 World Cup event winning streak, the German trio of Sylke Otto, Barbara Niedernhuber and Silke Kraushaar swept gold, silver and bronze, respectively. Otto, the 2000 and 2001 World Champion, led the way, racing to a total time of 2:52.464.

Clive Mason/Getty Images

Mark Grimmette and Brian Martin celebrate winning the silver medal in the men's doubles luge event at Utah Olympic Park.

Becky Wilczak and her female teammates were pleased with two top-ten finishes in their first Olympic Winter Games.

Al Bello/Getty Images

"I don't know what to say, I can't believe it," Otto said. "Finally, I've made it and it was a long way to this gold medal. I'm totally happy." Niedernhuber, who also finished in the silver medal position in '98, finished .321 seconds behind her teammate, while Kraushaar, the defending Olympic Champion, was .401 seconds off the pace.

The three-member American squad, each first-time Olympians, led by Becky Wilczak (River Forest, Ill.) captured a pair of top-10 finishes.

"To compete in our first Olympic competition, in our home country, was very special," said Wilczak, whose fifth place finish matched Cammy Myler's fifth place showing from the 1992 Albertville, France Olympic Winter Games for the best-ever U.S. result. "Myself and my teammates gained a tremendous amount of experience that will help us to be even more successful four years from now." Wilczak's four-heat combined time of 2:54.254 trailed Otto by 1.790 seconds.

Ashley Hayden (Westborough, Mass.) raced to an eighth place finish and a time of 2:54.658.

"We'll get to the Germans someday," said Hayden. "They're 30, 32-years-old, and each one of us are only in our twenties. We're not that far behind them. I think in just a few more seasons, we'll be having the first press conference."

Courtney Zablocki (Highlands Ranch, Colo.) finished 13th. Her fourth heat time of 43.383 seconds set a new American track record.

The 1316-meter long Utah Olympic Park course lived up to its reputation as the world's fastest track. Approaching speeds of 90 miles per hour, sliders in all three disciplines combined to shatter track records 12 times during the five days of racing. Track records were broken three times in the women's singles event before Otto's third heat time of 42.940 established the current mark.

In the men's singles event, the track record was broken six times before Prock established the new mark of 44.271 during the third heat of competition.

The doubles' field shattered the track record on three occasions before Leitner and Resch's first heat total of 42.953 set the current mark.   usa 2002

89

Crowd favorite Picabo Street powers down the slope in the women's downhill final.

Mike Powell/Getty Images

Coming into the 2002 Olympic Games, the U.S. Ski and Snowboard Association set an aggressive goal to win 10 medals -- more than 60% greater than the all-time best of six in Nagano. At the end of the Olympic Games, it was 'Mission Accomplished,' with record Olympic performances in virtually every sport.

ALPINE

By Tom Kelly, U.S. Ski & Snowboard Association

The Alpine events were full of speed and surprises on the wings of record-breaking performances. They were also the coming-out party for a young Croatian who became the winningest champion in history with four medals, including three gold. It was also an Olympic Games where the French recorded strong finishes on the wings of their late teammate and friend Regine Cavagnoud, who was tragically killed after the opening race of the 2002 season.

But for many Americans, it was the dawning of Bode Miller, whose daring 'full gas' racing captured the hearts of the fans, and the Olympic finale for skiing great Picabo Street.

Despite the fact no skiers had previously raced the steep Grizzly and Wildflower courses on Snowbasin's Mt. Ogden in World Cup downhills, there was tremendous respect for the Bernard Russi-designed courses. In training runs the Americans looked strong: Daron Rahlves (Sugar Bowl, Calif.) was perfectly suited to the technical, twisty-turn course as he showed in the first official training run. The same was true for Picabo Street (Park City, Utah) as she nailed her first training run.

Race day dawned perfectly for Rahlves. Starting 17th, he knew whom he had to catch. Coming out of the steep start, Rahlves held a .04 lead into the flat transition where his race would be won or lost. Setting up for the Flintlock Jump, Rahlves came in high and tight, hitting a lip, which threw him more than 150-feet down the mountain, hands flailing. He landed the perilous jump, but his race was over - losing precious time in the air and falling a second back. Despite his technical prowess, it was time Rahlves could not make up, and he finished 16th. Austrian Fritz Strobl

Gary M Prior/Getty Images

Bode Miller celebrates after winning the silver medal in the men's combined event.

Bode Miller overcame a near-crash at 70 mph to win silver in the men's combined slalom event.

Mike Powell/Getty Images

took the gold with Norwegian Lasse Kjus silver and favorite Stephan Eberharter of Austria bronze.

The bright spot for the U.S. team turned out to be young Marco Sullivan (Squaw Valley, Calif.), a former Sprint Ski Racing Junior Ski Racer of the Year, who surprised even himself with ninth. Jake Fiala (Frisco, Colo.) was 27th and Scott Macartney (Redmond, Wash.) finished 29th.

Fate seemed to be shining on Picabo Street in her comeback from a post-Nagano crash. Sitting 16th in the seeding list, Street couldn't pick her own start number. But the random draw put her in second starting position - the same position from which she won gold in Nagano and silver nine years earlier in the World Championships. But the Gods took a rest on downhill day, with winds forcing a one-day delay. In the new starting list draw, Street ended up 26 -- a start number which would ultimately seal her fate.

It was a tough day for the Americans. Caroline Lalive (Steamboat Springs, Colo.) crashed during what appeared to be a bound-for-a-medal run. Jonna Mendes (Heavenly, Calif.) finished 11th with Kirsten Clark (Raymond, Maine) 12th. And Street, despite skiing a technically

strong run, found her 26th start position too late in the day to be effective. Despite her 16th place finish, she blew kisses to the crowd and left the stadium as she had arrived - as an Olympic champion.

France's Carole Montillet, inspired by the leadership always provided by the late Cavagnoud - when she was alive and now in her memory - was a surprise winner over Italy's favored Isolde Kostner and Austria's Renate Goetschl.

The alpine combined -- where the time is added from a high-speed downhill and the technical, zigzag slalom event -- was the original Olympic alpine event in 1936. Gretchen Fraser's 1948 silver was the only U.S. medal...until now.

Bode Miller came into the combined as a favorite. But in the downhill portion, Miller suddenly went out of control at nearly 70 mph. He miraculously pulled it out, but found himself 2.44 seconds out of the lead.

In the first of two slalom runs, Miller was 2.44 seconds behind leader Kjetil Andre Aamodt. It would take a perfect second run just to get close to a bronze. And Miller did just that -- a perfect run and fastest of the day to move all the way up to silver! Aamodt took gold,

(L-R) Bode Miller of the USA (silver), Stephan Eberharter of Austria (gold), and Lasse Kjus of Norway (bronze) celebrate after the men's giant slalom.

with Austrian Benjamin Raich bronze. Miller's teammate, Fiala, was 19th while Casey Puckett (Aspen, Colo.) went out in the slalom.

The women's combined was the beginning of a stellar run for 20-year-old Janica Kostelic of Croatia. A superstar a year earlier, Kostelic won eight slaloms en route to the World Cup overall and slalom titles on a creaky left knee. But she matched a strong downhill with a perfect slalom to take combined gold ahead of Goetschl, who picked up her second medal, and Germany's Martina Ertl, who won her country's only alpine medal of the Olympic Winter Games.

Lindsey C. Kildow (Vail, Colo.), the youngest member of the entire U.S. Ski and Snowboard delegation at 17, had the best finish since Gretchen Fraser's silver in 1948, finishing sixth.

The super G is a cross between the more serpentine giant slalom and the high-speed downhill. It was the final chance for a U.S. medal in the speed events, with hopes resting on World Champion Rahlves and Lalive, who ranked sixth in the world. But it wasn't to be. Rahlves

Marco Sullivan zooms down the hill during the men's downhill event.

Picabo Street awaits her score at the finish of the women's downhill final.

Lindsay Kildow in action above, finished sixth in the women's combined slalom.

Mike Hewitt/Getty Images

Facing page: Daron Rahlves flies over a hill in the men's downhill.

ended up eighth, while Lalive went out. Olympic rookie Thomas Vonn (Newburgh, N.Y.) finished ninth with Macartney 25th and Sullivan going out in the men's race. The U.S. women wound up with Clark 14th, Mendes 16th and Katie Monahan (Aspen, Colo.) 17th.

The men's gold went to Aamodt, Eberharter won silver, and Austrian Andreas Schifferer took home bronze. The women's race saw one of the few surprises of the Olympic Games, with unheralded Daniela Ceccarelli of Italy taking gold, Kostelic silver and Italian Karen Putzer bronze.

After 10 days of nearly perfect weather at Snowbasin for the speed events, weather would end up playing a bigger role in the technical events at Deer Valley Resort and Park City Mountain Resort, an hour south of Snowbasin.

The women's slalom pitted World Cup leader Laure Pequegnot of France against number-two-ranked Kristina Koznick (Burnsville, Minn.) and Sarah Schleper (Vail, Colo.). Morning dawned with a heavy snow mixing with the softened racing base -- not the hard, icy surface racers crave. Despite starting number three, Koznick battled through holes and ruts before going off course near the finish of the first run.

Schleper met a similar fate when she came out of a binding at the

top. The same thing happened to Tasha Nelson (Burnsville, Minn.) and Kildow finished in 32nd place. The gold went to Kostelic -- her third Olympic medal in 2002 -- with Pequegnot taking silver by a mere .07 and Sweden's Anja Paerson bronze.

The sun was shining the next day at Park City -- the day hometown hero Erik Schlopy had been waiting for. But Schlopy touched down twice on his first run of giant slalom, and decided to pass on the second run to save his energy. That left it to Bode Miller to put on the show. No U.S. man had won an Olympic medal in the giant slalom (Tom Corcoran's fourth in 1960 was as close as they'd gotten), and Miller was within striking distance after finishing the first run in seventh. The pack was so tightly knotted that any of the top-15 could have struck a medal.

Miller's second run brought back memories of his combined slalom a week earlier at Snowbasin -- absolute perfection.

"I left everything out there, I don't have any more," Miller said at the finish.

Just like his performance a week earlier, it was the fastest second run and enough to boost him to silver behind Eberharter. Eberharter's gold medal completed his 2002 collection, adding to silver and bronze, with Kjus getting a second medal with bronze. Americans Dane Spencer (Boise, Idaho) was 16th and Vonn was 17th.

Coming in, coaches figured the giant slalom would be the toughest event for the U.S. women, and it was. Koznick was 17th, Schleper 21st, Clark 26th and Alex Shaffer (Park City, Utah) 28th in a comeback race after nearly two years out with leg and back injuries. It was all Kostelic for her record third gold and fourth medal. The Croatian won by 1.32 seconds over Paerson, who won her second medal. Sonja Nef won bronze - the only alpine medal of the Games for Switzerland.

The stage was set for an historic finale for Miller. No American had ever won three Winter Olympic medals, and slalom was his best event. The steep, side hill course at Deer Valley was perfectly suited for him. Starting first in the opening run, Miller was second behind France's Jean-Pierre Vidal. But the margin was surmountable, and in typical Bode fashion, the 24-year-old superstar went

Gary M Prior/ Getty Images

Kirsten Clark checks her time in the women's super giant slalom.

Mike Powell/Getty Images

Kristina Koznick zips down the course in the women's giant slalom. She finished in 17th place in this event.

Picabo Street bursts out of the starting gate to begin her run in the women's downhill event. The downhill event has the longest course reaching the highest speeds. Designed by Swiss Olympic downhill champion Bernard Russi, the downhill course at Snowbasin has a 9,311-foot (2,838-meter) summit and an 2,890-foot (881-meter) vertical drop.

all-out in the second run.

"I had to go full gas," Miller said. "If I skied conservatively and ended up fourth or fifth, I couldn't live with that."

Just over a dozen gates into the second run, already moving well into the lead, Miller went off course. History would have to wait. In the end, Vidal took the gold ahead of countryman Sebastian Amiez. Although Brit Alain Baxter won the bronze, he would later be disqualified for failing a drug test.

Bode Miller's 2002 medals were truly historic -- the first ever for a U.S. man in both combined and giant slalom. And he became only the second American man to win two medals in one Olympic Winter Games (along with Tommy Moe from 1994) and only the third to win two in a career (along with Phil Mahre from 1980 and 1984).

Who knows what's in store for this growing U.S. Alpine Team in Torino.   usa 2002

Park City resident Erik Schlopy kicks up some powder in the men's slalom event.

FREESTYLE

By Juliann Fritz, U.S. Ski and Snowboard Association

The mountains of Deer Valley Resort were the backdrop to freestyle history as a crowd of more than 16,000 people, the largest ever for the sport, were witnesses to a revolution in freestyle skiing. The fans will never forget the amazing feats they saw, like Czech Republic skier Ales Valenta's quint-twisting triple that won him the gold, and 1998 Olympic mogul gold medalist Jonny Moseley's (Tiburon, Calif.) 'dinner roll,' a near inverted horizontal twist that brought awe-struck fans to their feet.

"What attracts me to this sport is the new and fun stuff," 26-year-old Moseley said. "When I do it [the 'dinner roll'] I get energized, more than when I do any other trick."

And that was evident when he landed the 'roll' in qualifications to a roaring crowd. In typical Moseley fashion, he jumped the fence to celebrate with fans.

The freestyle women also left their mark on the sport as Switzerland's Evelyne Leu set a new world record for a women's aerial score (203.16), and Alisa Camplin won the first women's winter gold medal for Australia.

Team USA had big shoes to fill after winning three of four gold medals in freestyle at the 1998 Nagano Olympic Winter Games, but they rose to the occasion with three first-time Olympians winning silver in front of a hometown crowd.

Mogul skier Shannon Bahrke (Tahoe City, Calif.), wearing her good luck glitter eye shadow, was the first to win a medal for the Americans at the 2002 Olympic Winter Games. She knew she had a near flawless run upon crossing the finish line, and waved her arms ecstatically with joy. Her score just had to hold up through the last four skiers, two of which were her teammates Hannah Hardaway (Moultonbourgh, N.H.) and four-time Olympian Ann Battelle (Steamboat Springs, Colo.). It stuck until the very last competitor came down, reigning world champion and World Cup leader, Norwegian Kari Traa.

"We've had World Cups, Gold Cups and training camps here, so I think that gave a huge advantage to us," Bahrke said. "Although, the biggest advantage is having my hometown fans here...all these Americans cheering for you. I'm so proud to be an American."

The men's mogul competition followed three days later and while Moseley had the fans roaring with his new move, it was teammate Travis Mayer (Steamboat Springs, Colo.) that

Shaun Botterill/Getty Images

The Wasatch Mountains provide the backdrop as silver medalist Joe Pack is caught mid-flight during the men's aerials event.

Clive Brunskill/Getty Images

1998 moguls gold medalist Jonny Moseley executes the "dinner roll," his signature trick for the 2002 Olympic Winter Games.

Doug Pensinger/Getty Images

Brenda Petzold concentrates on finishing a flip in the qualifying round of the women's aerials competition.

bumped him out of medal contention. Skiing last and pumped up by the crowd he heard at the start gate, Mayer had a fast and sound run securing him the silver just a few points behind gold medalist Finn Janne Lahtela.

"If you would have told me a few months ago that I would even make the Olympics, I wouldn't have believed you," Mayer said. "My original goal was to qualify for the World Cup...I have definitely exceeded my goals this season."

With two medals secured by the mogul skiers, it was now up to the aerialists to contribute to the cause. The four U.S. men were triumphant as they all qualified for finals with Eric Bergoust placing

first, Joe Pack (Park City, Utah) in third, Jeret Peterson (Boise, Idaho) in seventh and Brian Currutt (Park City, Utah) holding tenth place.

Finals took place on an overcast day and the U.S. men set out to claim the medals that many thought were theirs for the taking. In the end, however, only hometown hero Joe Pack stood on the podium.

Every competitor used his biggest jumps, mostly quad twisters (four twists with three flips) except for Czech Ales Valenta. The former circus performer performed a jump with five twists and three flips for only the second time ever in competition. Pack finished five points behind Valenta and celebrated with a round of air guitar in the finish corral.

Doug Pensinger/Getty Images

Brian Bahr/Getty Images

Brian Bahr/Getty Images

Olympic rookie Hannah Hardaway launches off a mogul on her way to a fifth-place finish.

Left: Reigning World Cup aerials champ Eric Bergoust tucks his arms in mid-flight during a qualifying round of the men's event.

Below: Travis Mayer is all smiles after winning the silver medal in the men's moguls event. Mayer was on skis at age two and competing at age six.

Jeremy Bloom does the helicopter in the final round of the men's moguls. Bloom is a wide receiver on the University of Colorado football team when he is not training on the moguls.

Brian Bahr/Getty Images

One last competitor remained, and the only question seemed to be which medal he would get. But this was not the day for 1998 gold medalist Eric Bergoust. He knew Valenta had a high score and he was faced with the dilemma of sticking a solid quad jump after Valenta's feat of a quint. Sadly, the extra speed and energy required came at the expense of his landing as he slapped back and lost the gold within seconds. The crowd was silent.

"We had a lot of big scores today," Bergoust said. "I had to go for it on that one and went for it a little too much...but I don't regret going for it. I wanted to be either first or last. Nothing else would do."

Hometown heroes and underdogs won the day for the U.S. Olympic Freestyle Team and fans all left satisfied with their Olympic experience in Salt Lake City. The journey continues and the U.S. team will still be the one to watch at the 2006 Olympic Winter Games in Torino, Italy. usa 2002

Mike Powell/Getty Images

Shannon Bahrke proudly poses with her women's moguls silver medal at The Canyons in Park City, Utah.

Brian Currutt finishes with a smile in the men's aerials freestyle skiing final at the Deer Valley Resort. Currutt finished his first Olympic showing in sixth place.

Mike Hewitt/Getty Images

The starting line of the men's 30km freestyle event. Andrew Johnson finished 22nd, the best U.S. 30km result since Bill Koch in 1984.

CROSS COUNTRY

By Doug Haney, U.S. Ski and Snowboard Association

Expectations were not lofty for the U.S. Cross Country Team, but they left Soldier Hollow with one of their best Games results in history. Top-15 finishes for both men and women, along with a fifth place relay finish, were among the best results of all time.

Olympic three-timers John Bauer (Duluth, Minn.) and Justin Wadsworth (Bend, Ore.) raised the bar for the U.S. team along with the power of two-time vets Carl Swenson (Boulder, Colo.) and Patrick Weaver (Bend, Ore.). Add in the trump card with an extremely talented group of young skiers in Torin Koos (Leavenworth, Wash.), Lars Flora (Anchorage, Alaska), Kris Freeman (Andover, N.H.) and Andrew Johnson (Greensboro, Vt.) and the U.S. Men's Team was rolling at Soldier Hollow.

U.S. Olympic legend Nina Kemppel (Anchorage, Alaska) stood as the lone veteran on the women's side, leading an equally skilled group of young skiers in Tessa Benoit (South Pomfret, Vt.), Kristina Joder (Landgrove, Vt.), Barb Jones (Bozeman, Mont.), Aelin Peterson (Anchorage, Alaska), Kikkan Randall (Anchorage, Alaska), Wendy Wagner (Park City, Utah) and Lindsey Weier (St. Paul, Minn.).

Johnson, 24, set the tone for the men on the first day of competition with a 22nd in the men's 30km freestyle, the best 30km result since Bill Koch in 1984. Sparked by the unexpected top-25, the men's team landed three in the elite group three days later as Bauer posted a 12th, with Weaver only a few slots back at 16th and 21-year-old Kris Freeman 22nd in the 15km classical. The result for Bauer was a new mark for the U.S. team and the highest cross country finish for the U.S. team in 26 years.

"It really felt like a local race," Bauer said. "The crowd was behind me the whole time, pushing me up the hills and making me want to go faster. I actually heard hundreds of people yelling my name out there and it wasn't just my mom and a bunch of friends! That's what the Olympics are all about."

Freeman, still amped from the 30km, notched another top-20 result with 15th in the 10km pursuit, while Bauer skied with strength into 20th on a day split by a 10km classic followed by 10km freestyle.

Then came the 4x10km relay. Bauer and Freeman had already posted career results, but third and fourth leggers Wadsworth and

Swenson had yet to enter the mix. At the close of the 94-minute race, the U.S. skiers were just 70 seconds shy of a medal and had notched the highest Olympic finish in U.S. history with fifth.

"I don't think that there are many guys out there at Freeman's age who can beat him," head coach Christer Skog said. "An individual top-15 in his first Olympics and being a part of the historic relay team is something that we couldn't have dreamed of. These guys have worked so hard for that race and they really skied like gold medalists."

Youth was the theme for the U.S. women with many fresh faces making their Olympic debut. Names to keep an eye on in the future are 19-year-old Kikkan Randall and Aelin Peterson. Peterson wasn't slated to be at the Olympic level until 2006, yet made a breakthrough the previous winter and found herself with a ticket to the big show. Other solid contenders for the U.S. future are Benoit and Joder, who are perfecting

Kris Freeman jockeys for position with Andreas Schluetter of Germany in the men's 4x10km relay. Team USA finished fifth, their highest placing in U.S. Olympic history.

Justin Wadsworth skis past American fans during his leg of the men's 4x10km relay.

Clive Brunskill/Getty Images

Adam Pretty/Getty Images

This page: The future looks bright for Wendy Wagner (top photo) and Tessa Benoit (bottom photo), both of whom competed in their first Olympic Winter Games in Salt Lake City. Wagner placed 23rd in the 20km classical event and Benoit came in 54th in the 10km.

Facing page: Three-time Olympian John Bauer digs in during the men's 50km individual event. His 12th place finish in the 15km was the highest finish for an American in an individual cross country event in 26 years.

Clive Mason/Getty Images

their sprints to become the team's specialists. Throw in Wagner, who posted a career best 23rd in the 30km and prospects look good for 2006.

"That was a huge race for me," Wagner said. "If I can post a top-25 in my first Olympics, just give me four years and I should be right up there in Italy, plus with all these great skiers coming up the ranks and getting some Olympic experience, we should be a solid contender in 2006."

Leading the charge for the women was Nina Kemppel, the first female cross country athlete to compete in four Olympic Winter Games. Set to be her last Games, Kemppel stole the show, as she not only posted her personal best, but the best individual Olympic finish ever for an American woman with 15th in the 30km classic on the last day of competition.

"That race was the hardest of my life," Kemppel said. "It all came from 15 years of hard training and I started thinking to myself 'Alright Nina, those are the last two hills of your Olympic career.'"

The U.S. team's proud coach was happy with the cross country team's performance and hopeful for the future.

"People shouldn't be so surprised that this team is near the top," Skog said. "These Olympics were important for the U.S. Cross Country Team. We have proven that we can ski with the best in the world and are one of the countries that everyone will be looking at in the future. These Games were only a preview of what's to come."

usa 2002

Alan "Airborn" Alborn flies over the Olympic Rings in the men's K90 individual ski jumping event.

SKI JUMPING

By Doug Haney, U.S. Ski and Snowboard Association

It may only be a matter of 10 to 12 feet off the ground, but ski jumping athletes reach speeds of 60 mph before springing up to 120-meters in the air and landing on a snowy pitch of around 38 degrees.

Sound exciting? The Olympic crowd thought so as thousands of people flooded the Utah Olympic Park for five days of world-class ski jumping competition.

Ski jumping is scored by a points system that is based on style and is awarded by five judges on the side of the hill who rank each jumpers performance by form, landing, and a formula for distance.

Set to be the first event of the 2002 Olympic Winter Games, the K90 qualifier was scheduled to launch before the Opening Ceremony with U.S. jumper and 1998 Olympic veteran Brendan Doran (Steamboat Springs, Colo.) wearing bib No. 1. Unfortunately, unfavorable conditions pushed the intro event to two days later.

"It would have been cool to be the first competitor in the 2002 Games, but it was just awesome to be there and to be competing at my second Olympics," Doran said. "There is something special about jumping in front of Americans that you don't get competing in Europe. It's an energy that I have never experienced."

At 22, Doran was the oldest member of a young American squad that included 21-year-old team leader and fellow 1998 veteran Alan Alborn (Anchorage, Alaska), 18-year-old Tommy Schwall (Steamboat Springs, Colo.), 17-year-old Brian Welch (Scarborough, Maine) and the youngest member of the 2002 U.S. Olympic team, Clint Jones (Steamboat Springs, Colo.).

Head Coach Kari Ylianttila began fielding this troupe of athletes when he entered the U.S. program in 1994. As a postmark on his hard work, the Olympic season produced the best Olympic results since 1984, as Alborn led the way for the U.S. flyers.

"This team was the youngest jumpers out there," Ylianttila said. "To have all these guys getting their first Olympic experience at such young ages can only be a plus for this program. The next time the

Harry How/Getty Images

A jumper launches from the ramp in the men's K120 team ski jump.

Al Bello/Getty Images

Brendan Doran from Steamboat Springs, Colo. sets his skis in a "V" formation in the men's K90 ski jumping event. At 22, Doran was the oldest member of the American ski jumping team.

Donald Miralle /Getty Images

Seventeen-year-old Clint Jones sails through the air at Utah Olympic Park.

107

NORDIC COMBINED

By Doug Haney, U.S. Ski and Snowboard Association

For 70 years, Rolf Monsen's ninth place finish in the Lake Placid Olympic Winter Games stood as the best-ever finish for an American nordic combined athlete. It only took Todd Lodwick (Steamboat Springs, Colo.) two days in February to surpass that mark with a seventh place finish in the inaugural nordic combined event of the 2002 Olympic Winter Games.

Nordic combined is a sport that pairs ski jumping with cross country skiing to produce some of the world's most well-rounded athletes. The sport is often referred to as "the decathlon of skiing" because it requires a skier to use two totally different muscle groups: explosiveness and strength for the take-off in jumping, then swiftness and endurance for cross country.

The key to winning: jump far and then ski fast. With the jumping portion serving as the staging for the ski side of the event, it is essential for an athlete to jump well in order to achieve a high starting position for the skiing portion.

Sitting in the seventh spot following the jumping portion of the K90 individual event, Lodwick entered the ski portion in good position to climb onto the podium for the first time in U.S. history. Right behind him in the eighth spot was his teammate Bill Demong (Vermontville, N.Y.) who was surging after winning the final World Cup before Olympic competition. Yet Lodwick's skis weren't with him and he was unable to gain any ground on the snow, though fortunately he didn't lose any either.

"That race was huge for me," Lodwick said. "I was shooting for the roof with a medal, but it really felt great to start the Olympics with the best finish in U.S. history. It was a victory for me and the U.S. Nordic Combined program."

Climbing six spots in the race was Johnny Spillane (Steamboat Springs, Colo.), who finished 32nd, while Matt Dayton (Breckenridge, Colo.) posted a strong ski time to move to 18th with Demong finishing 19th. Snagging the gold medal was Finland's Samppa Lajunen, followed by teammate Jaako Tallus. Germany's Felix Gottwald climbed eight spots to snag the bronze.

After high winds and snow postponed the team competition, a well-rested U.S. team took to the jumps on February 16 with a medal hunger that propelled them into the best team jumping performance in history as they charged into third. Demong's huge leap of 94.5-meters set his teammates into celebration and set the stage for the team relay, in which each member was to ski a 5km loop.

Robert Laberge/Getty Images

Three-time Olympian Todd Lodwick sails through the air at Utah Olympic Park. Lodwick finished in fifth place in the sprint event, the best Olympic finish for the U.S. Nordic Combined Team in history.

"I knew I had to focus on that last jump," Demong said. "I just went up there and said, 'I need a little extra.' The crowd helped out a lot as the fifth man out there and it was nothing but pure energy for our team."

Head coach Tom Stietz agreed, saying that sitting in the third spot was higher than they could have asked for.

"Each member of the team had to step up their game and they did it," Stietz said. "It was the greatest day in the history of U.S. Nordic Combined, but there will be better."

With two historic marks set, the team moved into the K120 sprint with a hunger for something bigger. Yet a tough day on the 120-meter big hill

Mike Hewitt/Getty Images

Todd Lodwick, a native of Steamboat Springs, Colo., finished in seventh place in the individual nordic combined event.

Donald Miralle/Getty Images

Johnny Spillane finished the individual nordic combined event in 32nd place. Spillane started ski jumping at age 10.

Shaun Botterill/Getty Images

Todd Lodwick in action during the 7.5km sprint nordic combined event at Soldier Hollow. Lodwick would complete the ski portion and break the American record for best nordic combined finish with fifth.

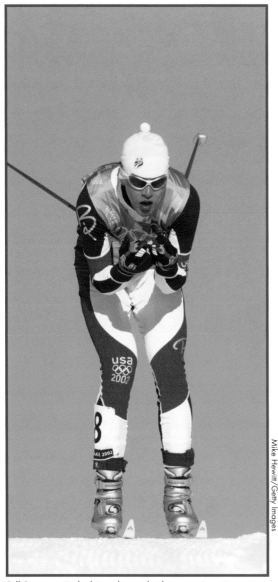

Mike Hewitt/Getty Images

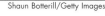

Donald Miralle/Getty Images

Bill Demong tucks his poles under his arms to gain speed. Demong finished 14th in the sprint event.

Olympic rookie Matt Dayton flies above photographers in the K90 individual nordic combined event.

left Lodwick in 12th, Demong only one spot behind, and Spillane and Dayton sitting 37th and 39th respectively.

A surprise call from Denver Broncos football legend John Elway to Lodwick one night earlier may have spurred him in the cross country segment of the sprint as he attacked the snow, hurdling seven skiers en route to a fifth place finish in the event. The result toppled his own seventh earlier in the Games as the best ever finish for a nordic combined American in Olympic history.

"I felt like I was one of the best in the world," Lodwick said. "I came into these Olympics sitting fourth in the World Cup standings with a chance to put the U.S. on the podium for the first time, but seventh, fourth and fifth in these Olympic Games -- there's nothing that I can be disappointed with."

Demong ended a career Olympics in 14th in the sprint, while Spillane climbed five spots to finish 32nd and Dayton jumped three to round out the U.S team with 36th. Finland's Lajunen capped a brilliant Olympic Winter Games with his third straight gold, sweeping all of the nordic combined events. He went into the cross country ski race leading by 15 seconds, and finished the race nine seconds in front of Germany's Ronny Ackermann, who won the silver. Gottwald of Austria nabbed the bronze after starting the race one slot ahead of Lodwick.

"These Olympics have been so great, not only with the crowd, but with family and friends who have come out to support the U.S. team," Lodwick said. "It really is surreal to look around and see the crowd with U.S. flags and screaming for everybody. That's what makes it so special." usa 2002

Silhouetted by the sun, a skier sails through the air in the K90 individual nordic combined event.

Ezra Shaw/Getty Images

SNOWBOARD

By Scott Flanders, U.S. Ski and Snowboard

So where do we go from here? That was the question floating around Park City Mountain Resort during the 2002 Olympic Winter Games after the U.S. Snowboard squad dominated, winning five total medals, including a clean sweep in the men's halfpipe event.

One of the more anticipated events of the Games, it was hard to believe that snowboarding was making just its second appearance as an Olympic medal sport. One look around the venue -- which was sold out all week -- and one would have thought the sport had made its debut at the first Winter Games back in 1924 in Chamonix, France.

The hoopla began with the women's halfpipe event. Three Americans earned the chance to ride for their country, including Kelly Clark (Mount Snow, Vt.), Shannon Dunn-Downing (Carnelian Bay, Calif.) and Tricia Byrnes (Stratton Mountain, Vt.).

Clark, who was in second place following the first of two runs in the finals, stepped it up in her final run and laid down a perfect pass full of intensity. She threw huge air after huge air, including a McTwist (inverted 540) and a frontside 720, all the while keeping it stylish.

Top: Vermont native Ross Powers bested his 1998 bronze with Salt Lake gold in the halfpipe competition.

Facing page: The camera catches an airborne Kelly Clark during her gold medal-winning performance in the women's halfpipe.

Below: Liver transplant survivor Chris Klug celebrates his bronze medal in the men's parallel giant slalom.

Donald Miralle/Getty Images

Al Bello,/Getty Images

Adam Pretty /Getty Images

Lisa Kosglow leans into a turn in the women's parallel giant slalom snowboard event. Kosglow was the top female American finisher with eighth.

Left: Jarret "JJ" Thomas catches air in the men's halfpipe. He would go on to complete the American sweep of the event by taking home the bronze.

Below: Halfpipe snowboarders Danny Kass (silver), Ross Powers (gold), and Jarret Thomas (bronze) pose proudly with their medals and the snowboards that carried them to victory in 2002.

Mike Powell/Getty Images

Danny Kass flies above the sold-out crowd in the final round of the men's halfpipe snowboard event. The little town of Park City became so crowded during the 2002 Olympic Winter Games, spectators had to park seven miles away and take buses to the venues.

The moments after Clark's second run were tense while the judges tallied her score. France's Doriane Vidal had just posted a 43.0, which looked tough to top. Then, the huge scoreboard lit up with four numbers: 47.9 for Clark's score and a 1 for her placing. The Vermonter had won America's first gold medal of the 2002 Games and the first snowboard gold for the U.S. in Olympic history.

Dunn-Downing, who had won bronze at the 1998 Nagano Games, finished fifth and Byrnes placed sixth, as Vidal won the silver and Swiss rider Fabienne Reuteler took bronze.

Fueled by Clark's amazing gold medal performance, the fans and the U.S. men went into the halfpipe contest with high expectations. Tommy Czeschin (Mammoth Lakes, Calif.), Danny Kass (Hamburg, N.J.), Ross Powers (South Londonderry, Vt.) and Jarret "JJ" Thomas (Golden, Colo.) were stoked to rip apart the Park City superpipe.

Powers, the lone American man with Olympic experience (he won bronze in 1998), absolutely killed it in his first run in the finals and laid down a score of 46.1. A typical Powers' run, it consisted of crazy big airs at the top, a perfect McTwist, and his trademark switch McTwist.

"The first two hits were the biggest airs I've ever done," Powers said. "Probably some of the biggest hits that have ever been done in pipe."

The airs were big enough to scare most people in the stands, and his score was big enough to scare the rest of the competitors. In fact, it was so big, it earned him a well-deserved gold medal.

As if Powers' gold wasn't enough, Kass won the silver and comeback kid Thomas took the bronze back to Colorado with him. Kass' runs were super technical and he earned the highest score of the day from the rotations judge. That was a no-brainer as he was pulling flawless Cab 1080s (coming in backwards, spinning three full rotations and landing backwards).

Thomas came from behind to win his bronze. He flailed in his first finals run, but went all out in his second, throwing his now-patented immense McTwist, a couple of huge tail grabs and a switch McTwist.

"The sweep was huge," Powers said. "To have Danny and JJ right there...the U.S. sweep, after everything that's happened in the States, is huge for us. Snowboarding started in the States, and to sweep it here in our home country, it's awesome for sure."

The state of Vermont, which already had deep roots in the sport of snowboarding, added Powers and Clark to a list of state highlights that includes maple syrup and the rock band Phish.

"Vermont must be psyched," Powers said. "I remember last time when I got the bronze, everyone there was just overwhelmed, and this time it's going to be crazy to go home. I'm just psyched I can do it again and go back and hang with everyone there."

Ironically, what may have been the best superpipe ever built was

SPEEDSKATING

Casey FitzRandolph proudly carries the American flag after winning the gold with a new Olympic record time of 34:42 during the men's 500-meter speedskating event.

Jamie Squire/Getty Images

LONG TRACK

By Nick Paulenich, U.S. Speedskating

The United States Long Track Speedskating Team entered the 2002 Salt Lake Olympic Winter Games with high hopes. The skaters were in top form and the track was reputed to be the fastest in the world. They did not

disappoint, tying the American team record set at the 1980 Olympic Winter Games in Lake Placid, N.Y., and setting numerous American, Olympic, and world records along the way.

Derek Parra won the team's first medal by claiming silver in the men's 5,000-meters. Parra crossed the line with a world record time of 6 minutes 17.98 seconds, eclipsing his previous personal best by nearly 15 seconds. Twenty-seven

Gary M. Prior/Getty Images

Derek Parra on his way to the silver medal during the men's 5000-meter speedskating event at the Utah Olympic Oval in Salt Lake City, Utah.

Al Bello/Getty Images

Gold medalist Chris Witty (left) and bronze medalist Jennifer Rodriguez pose for the cameras after the flower ceremony for the women's 1000-meter speedskating event.

minutes later, the Netherlands' Jochem Uytdehaage topped Parra by over three seconds to earn the gold medal.

"To have the world record, before it was taken away, was rewarding," Parra said. "I'm sure the Dutch at home watching television are saying 'No, this can't be right!' I'm just enjoying the moment. This is a total surprise."

Casey FitzRandolph set a world record in his first 500-meter race, skating a time of 34.42 seconds. The second day, FitzRandolph turned a time of 34.81 for a two-race total of 69.23 seconds to win the gold. Kip Carpenter took home the bronze with a time of 69.47.

"I knew coming into this weekend what I was capable of," FitzRandolph said. "I think the nerves were showing up a bit, and I didn't have exactly the race I wanted. Watching the other guys race today, they were confirming what I already knew, and that was I controlled my own destiny."

Competing in his first Olympic Games, Carpenter surprised himself by simply reaching the podium.

"I had no expectation of winning that medal going into my first Olympic event," he said. "Everything happened, it fell into place and it's a dream come true."

The American men placed all four skaters in the top seven of the 1000-meter competition. Joey Cheek led the way with a time of 1 minute 7.61 seconds.

"I was shocked, but thrilled. It was unbelievable," Cheek said. "I'm honestly pretty surprised. After I got done, I looked at the times, and saw my time...I never thought it would stand up to Jeremy (Wotherspoon, of Canada) or Erben (Wennemars, of the Netherlands). I was sure those guys were going to smoke it."

They didn't, and Cheek took home the bronze. Fourth place was occupied by Carpenter, who skated a time of 1:07.89. Nick Pearson placed sixth with a time of 1:07.97 while FitzRandolph was seventh with a time of 1:08.15.

Parra added a gold medal to his silver on February 19 as he skated a world record time of 1:43.95 in the 1500-meters. This time it was Uytdehaage who finished second. The race held extra meaning for Parra. The race was the first time in Salt Lake City that his wife, Tiffany, was in the stands. She works in Florida while he trains in Utah, and the couple gave birth to a baby girl, Mia, in December.

"When I go home at night, I'm in my room and the lights are off and I'm ready to go to bed, it's all I think about that I'm not there with my pregnant wife and now my

Kip Carpenter holds off a competitor during his skate to the bronze medal in the men's 500-meter long track event.

new baby," Parra said. "It is the hardest thing about being away. I saw her up in the stands before the race, and I kept telling her I love her. We've been apart for so long. For her to come here and see this race with my (whole family) for this moment, I'm thankful she got to be here."

The medal also made Parra the first Hispanic-American to ever earn gold at the Olympic Winter Games.

Parra and Jason Hedstrand skated in the 10,000-meters. Hedstrand was the top American, finishing 12th with a time of 13 minutes 32.99 seconds, a new American record. Parra finished directly behind him with a time of 13:33.44.

Uytdehaage claimed his second gold of the Games and third medal overall with a time of 12:58.92. The time was the first ever sub-13 minute performance in the 10,000-meters.

"I really went for it, and I've got to be pleased with that," Uytdehaage said. "I didn't hold anything back. It's the Olympics. There's no better time to lay it on the line. I've got no regrets about my race. I just wish my last couple of laps could have been faster."

Chris Witty and Jennifer Rodriguez led the U.S. women, combining for three medals.

Witty turned in one of the most memorable performances of the Salt Lake Games. Less than a month after being diagnosed with mononucleosis, Witty eclipsed the world record in the 1000-meters en route to a gold medal.

"(Even) if I was healthy, that (time) would have been a surprise," Witty said. "Regardless of the result, it was a dream race today."

Rodriguez also medaled, picking up a bronze with her time of 1:14.24. But with just one pair left to skate after her, she worried her time would not hold up.

"First I was crying that I didn't get a medal and then I was crying because I did," she said. "I went through the whole rainbow."

Rodriguez's second medal of the Salt Lake Games was a bronze medal in the 1500-meters.   She posted a time of 1:55.32 to finish behind the German duo of Anni Friesinger (1:54.02) and Voelker (1:54.97).

"I'm happy, I'm relieved, I'm glad it's over," Rodriguez said. "I think I put the most pressure on myself in this race, and I didn't care what color (the medal) was, I just wanted to be on the podium, and I was."

Witty put up a personal best of 1:55.71 and placed fifth in the 1500m. Amy Sannes was eighth (1:56.29) while Becky Sundstrom was 13th

Donald Miralle/Getty Images

Casey FitzRandolph won gold and set a new Olympic record with a time of 34.42 seconds in the men's 500-meter long track speedskating event.

(1:57.33). Rodriguez and Witty also posted solid performances in the 3000- and 500-meter events, respectively.   Rodriguez set an American record in the 3000 en route to posting a seventh-place finish with a time of 4:04.99.   The race was won by Germany's Claudia Pechstein, who recorded a time of 3:57.70-a new world record.

Witty skated her personal best in the 500-meters with a time of 38.36 seconds in her second race. Her two-race total of 76.73 seconds placed her 14th as Canada's Catriona LeMay Doan captured her second straight gold medal in the event with a total time of 74.75.

In the 5000-meters, U.S. competitors included Catherine Raney and Annie Driscoll. Raney set an American record of 7:06.89 and came in ninth, while Driscoll placed 14th with a time of 7:35.23.

"It exceeded all of my expectations by far," Raney said of the race. "I was just going out there to try and get a personal best."

Pechstein claimed the gold medal, breaking a world record and posting a time of six minutes, 46.91 seconds.

The eight medals earned by the United States tied Germany and the Netherlands for most medals in the discipline. The three countries combined for 24 of the 30 possible medals at the Utah Olympic Oval.   ⁓usa⁕2002

Adam Pretty/Getty Images

Catherine Raney set a new American record of 7:06.89 in the women's 5000-meter long track speedskating event.

Top left: Nick Pearson missed a medal placing in the men's 1000-meters by 0.3 seconds.

Top right: Joey Cheek celebrates his bronze medal-winning performance in the men's 1000-meter event.

Middle: Jennifer Rodriguez, seen here competing in the women's 3000-meter long track event, took home two bronze medals at the 2002 Olympic Winter Games.

Bottom: The determination shows in two-time Olympian Marc Pelchat's face as he races in the men's 500-meter event.

Chris Witty skates around a turn in the 1000-meter long track speedskating event. Witty, who was still suffering from mononucleosis, won the gold medal and broke records in a new World and Olympic record time of 1:13.83.

AP Photo/Lionel Cironneau

Apolo Anton Ohno of the United States holds up his gold medal during the ceremony for the men's 1,500-meter short track speedskating event.
Previous page: Apolo Anton Ohno leads the pack in the men's 1000-meter short track event.

SHORT TRACK

By Nick Paulenich, U.S. Speedskating

The short track speedskating competition proved to be one of the hottest tickets in Salt Lake City as 19-year-old phenomenon Apolo Anton Ohno quickly became one of the marquee names of the 2002 Olympic Winter Games. Analysts and the press had him marked for four medals, but Ohno had to settle for two because as they say in the sport, "That's short track!"

Ohno's first medal of the Salt Lake Games came in the 1000-meter event. With Ohno leading the race and heading toward the finish line, Ohno got tangled up with three other skaters nearing the finish line. The skaters went sprawling to the ice and Australian Steven Bradbury, who was well behind the pack and was left as the only skater standing, skated across the finish line for the gold medal. Ohno watched helplessly as Bradbury crossed the finish, tried to scramble to his feet, but was only able to crawl to the finish for the silver. Canadian Mathieu Turcotte was able to untangle from the wreckage to cross the line for the bronze.

"I could feel it, the win, in my fingers," Ohno said. "The next thing I knew, I was in the boards. I never take a race for granted until I've crossed the finish line."

Ohno sustained an injury to his left inner thigh from his own skate during the crash. The three-centimeter cut required six stitches, but Ohno's gutsy crawl to the finish captured the hearts of Olympic fans worldwide.

"It happens in short track, and this is the sport I live for," he said. "I got on the ice, and I was definitely very happy with (my) performance. Next time, I'll be a little farther in front."

Mathieu Turcotte #319 of Canada crashes into Apolo Anton Ohno #369 of the USA and Hyun-Soo Ahn #348 of Korea as they compete in the men's 1000-meter short track event. Steven Bradbury of Australia (not pictured) crossed the finish line first to win the gold medal.

Mike Hewitt/Getty Images

Apolo Anton Ohno of the USA backs off the elbow of Dong-Sung Kim of Korea in the last turn of the men's 1500-meter short track final. Kim was disqualified for obstructing the lane.

Adam Pretty/Getty Images

Ohno's teammate Rusty Smith reached the quarterfinals of the 1000-meters before being eliminated. Smith set an Olympic record in the opening heat of the event with a time of 1 minute 28.183 seconds, but Turcotte broke the short-lived record with a time of 1:27.185.

By the third night of short track competition, Ohno mania was reaching its peak as fans in the Salt Lake Ice Center carried signs for Ohno and wore stick-on "soul patches" to mimic the growth of hair on Ohno's chin.

After cruising through preliminary rounds of the 1500-meter event, Ohno reached the final. In the final, Ohno skated a relaxed, slow-paced race even through the first half of the final. In the last five laps, Ohno performed his signature speed passes and moved just behind the leader, Korea's Dong-Sung Kim. But this time, Ohno's last-lap-come-from-behind pass didn't happen. He tried on the inner lane, but a block from Kim saw Ohno cross the finish line in second. As Kim began his victory lap,

the official announced Kim had been disqualified for cross-tracking. Ohno had won his first Olympic gold medal.

"I came here, and I did an excellent job," he said. "So many people supported me -- all my friends and family in the stands, and that's just an unbelievable feeling. My first Games and I got two medals...there's nothing better than that."

Ohno finished the race in two minutes, 18.541 seconds. Chinese skater Jiajun Li claimed silver behind Ohno, and Canada's Marc Gagnon took bronze.

"I got to skate with the best, once again, and I got to go out there and perform for my country," he said. "In itself, it's just something that deep down in my heart, I'll keep forever."

Smith, who battled a severe cold, was unable to reach the final after being knocked out in the semifinals. Smith rebounded to finish first in the 1500-meter "B" final.

Smith was the surprise American medalist in the 500-meter event after Ohno was disqualified for impeding in the semifinals. Smith earned a bronze medal on the final night of short track behind Canadians Marc Gagnon and Jonathan Guilmette who won gold and silver medals, respectively. Gagnon broke the standing Olympic record and skated the 500 meters in 41.802 seconds.

"I'm so excited and so happy," Smith said. "Everything just worked out really well today. I had a great start, but I held the lead for a little too long, I think. But I'm really happy about the way things turned out."

Ohno and Smith teamed up with Ron Biondo and Dan Weinstein to compete in the 5000-meter relay. The quartet moved into the final by winning the semifinal heat, but another medal eluded the American team. With 27 laps to go, Smith caught his skate boot on one of the turning blocks and took a tumble. Despite their effort to catch back up, the American men finished fourth behind Canada (gold), Italy (silver) and China (bronze).

"It's hard to have a really good moment, then a really bad moment back to back," Smith said. "But I think my teammates understand that this is just part of the sport, and it's happened to all of us."

Mike Powell/Getty Images

Rusty Smith lead in the beginning of the 500-meter event, but settled for bronze when he was passed by Canadians Marc Gagnon (gold) and Jonathan Guilmette.

Three-time Olympic medalist Amy Peterson competes in the women's 1500-meter short track speedskating semifinal round. This marked her final Olympic Winter Games.

Robert Laberge/Getty Images

Although the American women did not do as well as the men, they skated hard and had the support of the home crowd. For Amy Peterson, it marked the fifth and final time she would compete in an Olympic Winter Games. The three-time Olympic medalist was the flagbearer for the United States in the Opening Ceremony.

In the 1500-meters, Peterson reached semifinal action before being eliminated.

"The competition has always been tough, but I think it's kind of moved along with the times," Peterson, who suffers from chronic fatigue syndrome, said. "Eight years ago, I probably had a different outlook than I have now. This year has just been kind of a struggle for me. Once I fell off the pace, I knew the race was over."

Peterson's teammate and training partner Erin Porter was disqualified in the first round after touching the skate of Japanese skater Yuka Kamino.

"I felt all the moves I made were the right moves," Porter said. "I'm not shocked. It's short track. I've had plenty of things (like this) happen to me."

Gi-Hyun Ko of Korea took the gold and was followed by her countrywoman Eun-Kyung Choi. Evgenia Radanova of Bulgaria finished with bronze.

Peterson and Caroline Hallisey competed next in the 500-meters. Peterson failed to qualify after the quarterfinal round, but Hallisey managed a race to the finals after a qualifying tie with Canadian Isabelle Charest in the semifinals. Hallisey's semifinal time of 44.307 seconds is a new American record.

Hallisey skated well in the finals and finished fifth overall.

Yang Yang (A) captured the first Winter Olympic gold medal for China with a time of 44.187.

The U.S. women's relay team -- Hallisey, Peterson, Porter, and Julie Goskowicz -- failed to qualify for the A final and thus competed in the B final of the 3000-meter relay. The team placed third behind Italy and Bulgaria. The race, Peterson's final Olympic appearance, set a new American record in the B final with a time of 4 minutes 20.730 seconds.

"It wasn't really that important, the placing," Peterson said. "We would have liked to have won the race, but we were in the mix of things, and we had a lot of fun just being in the race. We skated an American record, and that was important."

Hallisey raced in the first heats of the 1000-meters but did not qualify for advancement to the quarterfinals. In a difficult heat including gold medalist-to-be Yang Yang (A) of China, Hallisey said she was happy with her performance.

"I set a personal best. I'm extremely happy with that," she said. "To be able to hang on with Yang (A) and Korean skater Gi-Hyun Kim as long as I did is just more than I could have asked for. To get a chance to skate in the Games and have the results I had, I can't walk away unhappy."

Overall, the 2002 Olympic Winter Games were great for short track. Team USA's Ohno took home the first silver and gold medals ever for an American male, and at the same time brought in lots of new short track fans across the world.

Watch out for Team USA in Torino 2006! ⌐usa⌐2002

Donald Miralle/Getty Images

Left: Eun-Kyung Choi of Korea leads Caroline Hallisey of the USA in the women's 1000-meter short track heats. Both advanced to the next round.

Right: Erin Porter of the USA leads the pack during her heat in the women's 1500-meter short track preliminary round. Porter was disqualified for crashing into Yuka Kamino of Japan.

MEDALS

Clive Brunskill/Getty Images

(L-R) Danny Kass (silver), Ross Powers (gold), and Jarret Thomas (bronze), receive their medals in the men's halfpipe snowboard event. The medal sweep by the U.S. men was the first in Olympic history since 1956.

Clive Mason/Getty Images

Tristan Gale kisses the gold medal she won in the inaugural women's skeleton event.

Dedication • Commitment

Kelly Clark celebrates her gold medal from the women's halfpipe snowboard event. Clark won the first U.S. gold medal during the 2002 Olympic Winter Games.

Michelle Kwan smiles while the National Anthem plays after winning the bronze medal in ladies' figure skating.

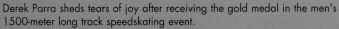

Derek Parra sheds tears of joy after receiving the gold medal in the men's 1500-meter long track speedskating event.

(L-R) Marc Gagnon (bronze) of Canada, Apolo Anton Ohno (gold) of the USA, and Jiajun Li (silver) of China, look on as the flags are raised for the men's 1500-meter short track speedskating event. Ohno's gold was the first U.S. men's gold medal in short track.

Al Bello/Getty Images

Doug Pensinger/Getty Images

Above: Bode Miller savors his silver medal in the men's combined.   Miller also won silver in the giant slalom ski event.

Left: Chris Klug yells to the crowd after receiving his bronze medal in men's snowboard parallel giant slalom.

Bottom left: Timothy Goebel proudly displays his bronze medal to the crowd. Goebel won the medal in men's figure skating.

Bottom right: Hometown hero Joe Pack receives his silver medal for the men's freestyle aerials ski event.

Al Bello/Getty Images

Ezra Shaw/Getty Images

Elsa/Getty Images

(L-R) Hiroyasu Shimizu of Japan (silver), Casey FitzRandolph (gold), and Kip Carpenter (bronze), receive their medals for the men's 500-meter long track speedskating event.

Al Bello/Getty Images

Mark Grimmette and Brian Martin proudly watch the Amercan flag being raised in their honor after receiving their silver medals in the men's doubles luge.

Hard Work • Sacrifice • Victory

Joey Cheek poses with his bronze medal from the men's 1000-meter long track speedskating event.

SALT LAKE 2002

(L-R) Sabine Voelker (silver) of Germany, Chris Witty (gold), and Jennifer Rodriguez (bronze), all receive their medals for the women's 1000-meter speedskating event.

Dedication • Commitment

Clive Mason/Getty Images

Lea Ann Parsley receives her silver medal won in the inaugural women's skeleton event. The U.S. Skeleton Team won three medals in 2002.

The U.S. men's silver and bronze four-man bobsleigh teams proudly pose with their medals at the medal awards ceremony in downtown Salt Lake City.

John Gichigi/Getty Images

Doug Pensinger/Getty Images

Sarah Hughes poses for photographers with her parents John and Amy Hughes after winning the gold medal in the ladies' figure skating event.

Jamie Squire/Getty Images

The U.S. Hockey Team played hard in 2002 and won silver, a vast improvement over their performance in Nagano.

Dedication • Commitment

Clive Mason/Getty Images

Clive Mason/Getty Images

Top left: Third generation Olympian Jim Shea rejoices after receiving his gold medal in men's skeleton.

Top right: A teary-eyed Vonetta Flowers and Jill Bakken watch the American flag being raised after receiving their gold medals in the inaugural women's bobsleigh event.

Bottom left: Travis Mayer puts his hand over his heart after being awarded a silver medal in the men's freestyle moguls ski event.

Bottom right: Rusty Smith receives the home crowd's adulation after receiving his bronze medal in the men's 500-meter short track event.

Donald Miralle/Getty Images

Donald Miralle/Getty Images

Gary M. Prior/Getty Images

Mike Hewitt/Getty Images

Shannon Bahrke is in awe after receiving her silver medal in the women's freestyle moguls ski event.

Apolo Anton Ohno celebrates receiving the silver medal in the men's 1000-meter short track speedskating event. Ohno would go on to win the gold in the 1500-meter event.

AP Photo/Dusan Vranic

Clay Ives and Chris Thorpe receive their bronze medals in the men's doubles luge at the Olympic Medals Plaza in Salt Lake City, Utah.

Dedication • Commitment

Robert Laberge/Getty Images

Chris Witty waves to the crowd at the Olympic Medals Plaza. Witty won her gold medal for the women's 1000-meter long track speedskating event.

Robert Laberge/Getty Images

Team USA waves to the crowd after receiving their silver medals in women's ice hockey.

Hard Work • Sacrifice • Victory

145

AMERICAN SPIRIT

Several generations of this Utah family wait patiently for the Torch Relay to pass and see their American flag.

Gary Bogden/Orlando Sentinel

Brian Bahr/Getty Images

Bronze medalist Brian Shimer carries the American flag during the Closing Ceremony.

Brian Bahr/Getty Images

A young fan of Team USA observes the men's hockey game between Belarus and the USA.

Picabo Street fan Andy Confin from Layton, Utah wraps his disappointment in his American flag after the cancellation of the women's downhill.

USA fans wave the flag as Team USA enters the ice before their game against Germany. The U.S. women won, 10-0.

A fan looks on at the Opening Ceremony.

A fan holds up a patriotic sign at the Opening Ceremony. The photo on the sign is of firefighters at Ground Zero raising a flag they found in the rubble. One of seven of the flags found at Ground Zero was brought into the Opening Ceremony of the 2002 Olympic Winter Games.

Fans of the USA Women's Hockey Team cheer after a goal in the second period of a preliminary round game against China.

Jim Shea jumps into the crowd of American fans after winning the gold medal in the men's skeleton event.

Fans in crazy wigs cheer as they watch the final round of the men's halfpipe snowboard event.

A USA fan is caught talking on his cell phone during the USA vs. Canada men's ice hockey gold medal match.

Shaun Botterill /Getty Images

A USA fan wrapped in a patriotic scarf watches the women's bobsleigh event.

Al Bello/Getty Images

Shirtless USA fans brave the cold during the final round of the men's moguls ski event.

A young fan cheers for Team USA during the women's hockey game against Finland.

Brian Bahr/Getty Images

Derek Parra wins the gold medal in a new World and Olympic record time of 1:43.95 in the men's 1500-meter long track speedskating event.

USA flags and Joe Pack signs dominate the crowd at the men's freestyle aerials skiing final.

Team USA walks off the ice surrounded by patriotic fans after their hockey game against Germany.

Flagbearer and short track speedskater Amy Petersen leads Team USA during the Opening Ceremony.

Rock singer Jon Bon Jovi, draped in an American flag, performs during the Closing Ceremony.

A message from a fan at the women's bobsleigh event. Jill Bakken and Vonetta Flowers went on to win the first gold in this new event.

Mike Hewitt/Getty Images

JOY & DESPAIR

Gina Ferozzi/LA Times

John Gichigi/Getty Images

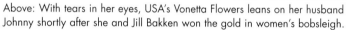

Above: With tears in her eyes, USA's Vonetta Flowers leans on her husband Johnny shortly after she and Jill Bakken won the gold in women's bobsleigh.

Top right: Australian freestyle skier Jacqui Cooper gets emotional during a press conference to talk about her knee injury. Cooper was picked to win gold, but injured herself in a training run prior to the women's aerials competition.

Bottom left: Sarah Hughes and coach Robin Wagner appear shocked to learn Hughes has won the gold in ladies' figure skating.

Bottom right: Simon Ammann of Switzerland is more than excited about winning gold in the individual K90 ski jumping event.

Jamie Squire/Getty Images

Brian Bahr/Getty Images

Doug Pensinger/Getty Images

Harry How/Getty Images

Gary Bogden/Orlando Sentinel

Top left: The U.S. men's ice hockey team celebrates a momentous 3-2 victory over Russia. The historic event occurred on the anniversary of their last meeting in 1980 when the U.S. team won the gold medal.

Top right: Alisa Camplin of Australia is in awe after winning the gold medal in women's freestyle aerials. Camplin was later shocked again when she learned that her family traveled from Australia to witness her performance, even though she asked them not to.

Middle: Hoping for gold in doubles luge, Brian Martin and Mark Grimmette anxiously watch the Germans slide down the track. The U.S. duo gratefully settled for silver, besting their Nagano bronze.

Right: Exhausted competitors collapse at the finish line of the men's 10km cross country free pursuit. Fulvio Valbusa of Italy (#31) had to jump over skiers and skis to finish the race.

Donald Miralle/Getty Images

Third generation U.S. Olympian Jim Shea Jr. holds a picture of his grandfather Jack Shea while hugging his mother after winning gold in men's skeleton.

Eric Bergoust falls while landing in the final round of the men's freestyle aerials event.

Chris Klug (left) hugs the crowd after winning bronze in the men's parallel giant slalom snowboard event, while fourth place finisher Nicolas Huet of France hangs his head in disappointment.

Erin Porter of the U.S. short track speedskating team collides with Nina Evteeva of Russia during the women's 1000-meter event.

Coach Bart Schouten congratulates a tearful Derek Parra who won the gold medal in World record time during the men's 1500-meter long track speedskating event.

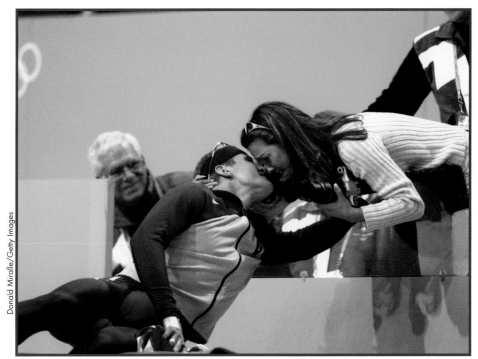

Gold medal winner Casey FitzRandolph kisses his girlfriend Jennifer Cocher after the men's 500-meter long track speedskating event.

Jenny Potter (#12) and Sarah Tueting (#29) of the U.S. women's ice hockey team react to Canada winning the gold medal game.

Dong-Sung Kim of Korea (right) throws his flag onto the ice after the announcement was made that he was disqualified. Ohno (left), won the gold medal in the 1500-meter short track event, due to Kim's disqualification for cross-tracking.

TORCH RELAY

An emotional President Bush comforts torchbearer Elizabeth Howe on the South Lawn of the White House. Howe's husband was a victim of the September 11 tragedy.

Todd Warshaw/Pool/Getty Images

Todd Warshaw/Pool/Getty Images

Torchbearer Dan Doctoroff pauses to look at the New York City skyline from his leg of the Torch Relay in Staten Island, New York.

Torchbearer George Dicarlo emerges from the water with the Olympic Flame at the Glenwood Springs Hot Springs pool in Colorado.

Children cheer on the Olympic Flame during the 2002 Salt Lake Olympic Torch Relay in Loveland, Colorado.

Torchbearer Oscar Black carries the Olympic Flame over the Coronado Bridge with San Diego, California in the background.

Torchbearer Richard Castaldo carries the Olympic Flame during the 2002 Salt Lake Olympic Torch Relay in Littleton, Colorado. Castaldo was injured in the 1999 Columbine High School shooting.

Todd Warshaw/Pool/Getty Images

Torchbearer Robin Creemer enjoys carrying the Olympic Flame during the 2002 Salt Lake Olympic Torch Relay in St. Louis, Missouri.

Todd Warshaw/Pool/Getty Images

Torchbearer Doug Santer carries the Olympic Flame at the Cowboy Hall of Fame in Oklahoma City, Oklahoma.

Todd Warshaw/Pool/Getty Images

Stephanie Spann carries the torch after receiving a Native American blessing at the Arches National Park in Moab, Utah.

Todd Warshaw/Pool/Getty Images

Todd Warshaw/Pool/Getty Images

Torchbearer Leonard Moon (right) greets his wife Delores before he passes the Olympic Flame to her during the 2002 Salt Lake Olympic Torch Relay in Manti, Utah.

A young fan celebrates as his mom carries the Olympic Flame during the 2002 Salt Lake Olympic Torch Relay in Garland, Utah.

Todd Warshaw/Pool/Getty Images

David Sanders/Arizona Daily Star

Tucson bicyclist Dwight Nelson rides up Gates Pass in Tucson, Arizona with the Olympic Flame.

167

EXECUTIVE COMMITTEE

Sandra Baldwin
Phoenix, Ariz.
(USOC President)

Robert Ctvrtlik
Huntington Beach, Calif.
(International Olympic Committee)

Anita L. DeFrantz
Los Angeles, Calif.
(International Olympic Committee)

Cedric Dempsey
Indianapolis, Ind. (Education-Based
Multisport Organization - NCAA)

Brian Derwin,
Apple Valley, Minn (Olympic/Pan
Am Sports Org. – USA Weightlifting)

Chris Duplanty
Newport Beach, Calif.
(Athletes' Advisory Council)

James L. Easton
Van Nuys, Calif.
(International Olympic Committee)

Herman R. Frazier
Birmingham, Ala.
(USOC Vice President)

Paul E. George
Wellesley, Mass.
(USOC Vice President))

Rachel Godino
Needham, Mass.
(Athletes' Advisory Council)

William J. Hybl
Colorado Springs, Colo.
(USOC Immed. Past Pres. and Pres.
Emeritus, IOC member)

James R. Joy
Triangle, Va.
(Armed Forces – U.S. Marine Corps)

Marty Mankamyer
Colorado Springs, Colo.
(USOC Vice President Secretariat)

Robert Marbut
San Antonio, Texas (Olympic/Pan
Am Sports Organization - U.S.
Modern Pentathlon)

Frank Marshall
Santa Monica, Calif.
(USOC Vice President Treasurer)

Mary McCagg
Cambridge, Mass.
(Athletes' Advisory Council)

Jim McCarthy
Chicago, Ill.
(Olympic/Pan Am Sports Organization
- U.S. Ski & Snowboard)

Albert Monaco Jr.
Lakeview, Ore.
(Olympic/Pan Am Sports
Organization - USA Volleyball)

Herb Perez
San Francisco, Calif.
(Athletes' Advisory Council)

Bill Stapleton
Austin, Texas
(USOC Vice President)

Rob Stull
Tampa, Fla.
(Athletes' Advisory Council)

Lisa Voight
Colorado Springs, Colo.
(Olympic/Pan Am Sports
Organization - USA Cycling)

Lloyd Ward
Colorado Springs, Colo.
(USOC Chief Executive Officer)

USA DELEGATION AND MISSION STAFF

Sandra Baldwin
USOC President
Phoenix, Ariz.

Dwight Bell
Chef de Mission
Atlanta, Ga.

Larry Buendorf
Security Director
Colorado Springs, Colo.

Francisco Campo
Asst. Delegation Director
Colorado Springs, Colo.

Greg Harney
Attaché/Managing Director
Colorado Springs, Colo.

Jim McCarthy
Asst. Chef de Mission
Chicago, Ill.

Mike Moran
Delegation Spokesperson
Colorado Springs, Colo.

Gary Moy
Delegation Director
Colorado Springs, Colo.

Heather Ross
Asst. Delegation Director
Colorado Springs, Colo.

Gale Tanger
Asst. Chef de Mission
Wauwatosa, Wis.

Lloyd D. Ward
USOC CEO/Secretary General
Colorado Springs, Colo.

USOC BOARD OF DIRECTORS

Tony Baggiano,
Alexandria, Va.

Dr. Gwendolyn C. Baker,
New York, N.Y.

Steven B. Baker,
Olathe, Kansas

Brenda Nichols Baldwin,
Windernere, Fla.

Sandra Baldwin,
Phoenix, Ariz.

William H. Bankhead,
Baton Rouge, La.

Kathy Beauregard,
Kalamazoo, Mich.

Nick A. Becker,
Newport Coast, Calif.

Dwight Bell,
Atlanta, Ga.

Rich Bender,
Colorado Springs, Colo.

Bret Bernard,
Manhattan Beach, Calif.

Roland Betts,
New York, N.Y.

Bill Bradley,
New York, N.Y.

Walter L. Bush Jr.,
Edina, Minn.

Michael Buss,
Indianapolis, Ind.

Keith Calkins,
Penn Valley, Calif.

Lynn Cannon,
Oroville, Calif.

Will Carlin,
Brooklyn N.Y.

Gary Castro,
Edmond, Okla.

Christopher Cole,
Flint, Mich.

Dr. S. Robert Contiguglia,
Denver, Colo.

Ron Creel,
Montgomery, Ala.

Bob Ctvrtlik,
Huntington Beach, Calif.

Donna Cunningham,
Amarillo, Texas

Doug Pensinger/Getty Images

SALT LAKE 2002

light the fire within

RESULTS

Biathlon

Women's 7.5km Sprint

Rank	Country	Athlete	Score/Time
1	GER	Kati Wilhelm	20:41.4
2	GER	Uschi Disl	20:57.0
3	SWE	Magdalena Forsberg	21:20.4
4	NOR	Liv Grete Poiree	21:24.1
5	FRA	Florence Baverel	21:27.9
6	RUS	Galina Koukleva	21:32.1
7	FRA	Sandrine Bailly	21:35.7
8	RUS	Olga Pyleva	21:44.2
49	USA	Kara Salmela	23:44.1
50	USA	Andrea Nahrgang	23:48.7
60	USA	Rachel Steer	24:41.7

Women's 4x7.5km Relay

Rank	Country	Athletes	Score/Time
1	GER	Apel, Disl, Henkel, Wilhelm	1:27:55.0
2	NOR	Skjelbreid, Tjoerhom, Andreassen, Poiree	1:28:25.6
3	RUS	Pyleva, Koukleva, Ishmouratova, Akhatova	1:29:19.7
4	BUL	Filipova, Nikoultchina, Karagiozova, Dafovska	1:29:25.8
5	SVK	Jasicova, Murinova, Pavkovcekova, Mihokova	1:30:11.5
6	SLO	Larisi, Grasic, Grudicek, Brankovic	1:30:18.0
7	BEL	Nazarova, Lysenko, Kutsepalova, Khrustaleva	1:31:01.6
8	CZE	Losmanova, Rezlerova, Cesnekova, Hakova	1:31:07.6
15	USA	Nahrgang, Salmela, Steer, Sabasteanski	1:41:16.0

Women's 10km Pursuit

Rank	Country	Athlete	Score/Time
1	RUS	Olga Pyleva	31:07.7
2	GER	Kati Wilhelm	+5.3
3	BUL	Irina Nikoultchina	+8.1
4	NOR	Liv Grete Poiree	+10.6
5	RUS	Galina Koukleva	+24.0
6	SWE	Magdalena Forsberg	+26.3
7	GER	Katrin Apel	+40.2
8	SLO	Andreja Grasic	+54.2
45	USA	Kara Salmela	+6:00.0
47	USA	Andrea Nahrgang	+7:00.8
60	USA	Rachel Steer	DNS

Women's 15km Individual

Rank	Country	Athlete	Score/Time
1	GER	Andrea Henkel	47:29.1
2	NOR	Liv Grete Poiree	47:37.0
3	SWE	Magdalena Forsberg	48:08.3
4	RUS	Olga Pyleva	48:14.0
5	BUL	Ekaterina Dafovska	48:15.5
6	BLR	Olga Nazarova	48:29.9
7	GER	Martina Glagow	48:34.2
8	RUS	Svetlana Ishmouratova	48:45.0
31	USA	Rachel Steer	51:50.6
55	USA	Kristina Sabasteanski	55:00.9
59	USA	Kara Salmela	57:25.9

Men's 10km Sprint

Rank	Country	Athlete	Score/Time
1	NOR	Ole Einar Bjoerndalen	24:51.3
2	GER	Sven Fischer	25:20.2
3	AUT	Wolfgang Perner	25:44.4
4	GER	Ricco Gross	25:44.6
5	AUT	Wolfgang Rottmann	25:48.8
6	RUS	Robert Rostovtsev	25:50.1
7	RUS	Victor Maigourov	25:50.9
8	NOR	Frode Andresen	25:51.5
20	USA	Jeremy Teela	26:36.6
26	USA	Jay Hakkinen	26:43.5
54	USA	Lawton Redman	27:43.4

Men's 12.5km Pursuit

Rank	Country	Athlete	Score/Time
1	NOR	Ole Einar Bjoerndalen	32:34.6
2	FRA	Raphael Poiree	+43.0
3	GER	Ricco Gross	+56.0
4	AUT	Ludwig Gredler	+1:00.9
5	RUS	Pavel Rostovtsev	+1:08.5
6	AUT	Wolfgang Rottmann	+1:10.5
7	RUS	Victor Maigourov	+1:20.5
8	NOR	Halvard Hanevold	+1:25.0
13	USA	Jay Hakkinen	+1:37.2
23	USA	Jeremy Teela	+2:43.5
52	USA	Lawton Redman	+6:24.4

Men's 20km Individual

Rank	Country	Athlete	Score/Time
1	NOR	Ole Einar Bjoerndalen	51:03.3
2	GER	Frank Luck	51:39.4
3	RUS	Victor Maigourov	51:40.6
4	GER	Ricco Gross	51:58.7
5	NOR	Halvard Hanevold	52:16.3
6	RUS	Pavel Rostovtsev	52:33.5
7	NOR	Frode Andresen	52:39.1
8	RUS	Serguei Tchepikov	52:44.2
14	USA	Jeremy Teela	53:56.5
26	USA	Jay Hakkinen	55:13.8
76	USA	Dan Campbell	54:58.6

Men's 4x7.5km Relay

Rank	Country	Athletes	Score/Time
1	NOR	Hanevold, Andresen, Gjelland, Bjoerndalen	1:23:42.3
2	GER	Gross, Sendel, Fischer, Luck	1:24:27.6
3	FRA	Marguet, Defrasne, Robert, Poiree	1:24:36.6
4	RUS	Maigourov, Rozhkov, Tchepikov, Rostovtsev	1:24:54.4
5	CZE	Garabik, Masarik, Dostal, Vitek	1:26:36.1
6	AUT	Sumann, Perner, Rottmann, Gredler	1:26:58.9
7	UKR	Derkach, Bilanenko, Pryma, Lysenko	1:27:02.2
8	BLR	Aidarov, Syman, Ryzhenkov, Sashurin	1:27:12.0
15	USA	Teela, Hakkinen, Campbell, Redman	1:30:27.1

Bobsleigh and Skeleton

Two-woman Bobsleigh

Rank	Country	Team	Score/Time
1	USA	Bakken - Flowers	1:37.76 TR
2	GER	Prokoff - Holzner	1:38.06
3	GER	Erdmann - Herschmann	1:38.29
4	SUI	Burdet - Sutter	1:38.34
5	USA	Racine - Johnson	1:38.73
6	NED	Jurg - Kiemel	1:39.18
7	ITA	Bellutti - Weissensteiner	1:39.21
8	RUS	Tokovaia - Bader	1:39.27

Two-man Bobsleigh

Rank	Country	Team	Score/Time
1	GER	Langen - Zimmermann	3:10.11
2	SUI	Reich - Anderhub	3:10.20
3	SUI	Annen - Hefti	3:10.62
4	USA	Hays - Hines	3:10.65
5	CAN	Lueders - Zardo	3:10.73
6	GER	Spies - Sagmeister	3:10.84
7	AUT	Stampfer - Schuetzenauer	3:11.16
8	ITA	Huber - Tartaglia	3:11.64
9	USA	Shimer - Steele	3:11.93

Four-man Bobsleigh

Rank	Country	Athletes	Score/Time
1	GER-2	Lange, Kuehn, Kuske, Embach	3:07.51
2	USA-1	Hays, Jones, Schuffenhauer, Hines	3:07.81
3	USA-2	Shimer, Kohn, Sharp, Steele	3:07.86
4	SUI-1	Annen, Schaufelberger, Hefti, Grand	3:07.95
5	FRA-1	Mingeon, Le Chanony, Fouquet, Arbez	3:08.56
6	SUI-2	Reich, Anderhub, Acklin, Aeberhard	3:08.59
7	LAT-1	Prusis, Rullis, Silarajs, Ozols	3:09.06
8	RUS-1	Popov, Makartchuk, Golubev, Stepuschkin	3:09.15

Women's Skeleton

Rank	Country	Athlete	Score/Time
1	USA	Tristan Gale	1:45.11
2	USA	Lea Ann Parsley	1:45.21
3	GBR	Alex Coomber	1:45.37
4	GER	Diana Sartor	1:45.53
5	SUI	Maya Pedersen	1:45.55
6	CAN	Lindsay Alcock	1:45.69
7	RUS	Ekaterina Mironova	1:45.95
7	GER	Steffi Hanzlik	1:45.95

Men's Skeleton

Rank	Country	Athlete	Score/Time
1	USA	Jim Shea	1:41.96
2	AUT	Martin Rettl	1:42.01
3	SUI	Gregor Staehli	1:42.15
4	IRL	Clifton Wrottesley	1:42.57
5	USA	Lincoln Dewitt	1:42.83
6	CAN	Jeff Pain	1:42.92
7	USA	Chris Soule	1:42.98
8	JPN	Kazuhiro Koshi	1:43.02

RESULTS

Curling

Women

Rank	Country	Athletes
1	GBR	Martin, Knox, MacDonald, Rankin, Morton
2	SUI	Ebnöther Ott, Frei,Bidaud, Röthlisberger-Raspe
3	CAN	Law, Skinner, Wheatcroft, Nelson, Noble
4	USA	Erickson, McCormick, Liapis, Swisshelm, Cotton
5	GER	Nesser, Belkofer, Wieländer, Stock, Fischer
6	SWE	Gustafson, Nyberg, Marmont, Persson, Bertrup
7	NOR	Nordby, Woods, Haslum, Holth, Løvseth
8	JPN	Katoh, Hayashi, Onodera, Konaka, Ishizaki
8	DEN	Bidstrup, Slotsager, Krause, Lund Nielsen, Richardson

Men

Rank	Country	Athletes
1	NOR	Trulsen, Vaagberg, Davanger, Ramsfjell, Nergaard
2	CAN	Martin, Walchuk, Rycroft, Bartlett, Tralnberg
3	SUI	Schwaller, Schwaller, Eggler, Grichting, Ramstein
4	SWE	Lindholm, Nordin, Swartling, Narup, Kraupp
5	FIN	Uusipaavalniemi, Mäkelä, Häti, Laukkanen, Saarelainen
6	GER	Stock, Herberg, Knoll, Messenzehl, Hoffman
7	DEN	Schmidt, Lavrsen, Hansen, Svensgaard, Gufler
7	GBR	McMillan, Smith, MacDonald, Loudon, Brown
7	USA	Somerville, Schneeberger, Brundidge, Gordon, Barcome

Figure Skating

Ladies'

Rank	Country	Athlete
1	USA	Sarah Hughes
2	RUS	Irina Slutskaya
3	USA	Michelle Kwan
4	USA	Sasha Cohen
5	JPN	Fumie Suguri
6	RUS	Maria Butyrskaya
7	CAN	Jennifer Robinson
8	HUN	Julia Sebestyen

Men's

Rank	Country	Athlete
1	RUS	Alexei Yagudin
2	RUS	Evgeni Plushenko
3	USA	Timothy Goebel
4	JPN	Takeshi Honda
5	RUS	Alexander Abt
6	USA	Todd Eldredge
7	USA	Michael Weiss
8	CAN	Elvis Stojko

Pairs

Rank	Country	Team
1	RUS	Berezhnaya - Sikharulidze
2	CAN	Sale - Pelletier
3	CHN	Shen - Zhao
4	RUS	Totmianina -Marinin
5	USA	Ina - Zimmerman
6	RUS	Petrova - Tikhonov
7	POL	Zagorska - Siudek
8	CZE	Berankova - Dlabola
13	USA	Scott - Dulebohn

Ice Dancing

Rank	Country	Team
1	FRA	Anissina - Peizerat
2	RUS	Irina Lobacheva - Averbukh
3	ITA	Fusar Poli - Margaglio
4	CAN	Bourne - Kraatz
5	LTU	Drobiazko - Vanagas
6	ISR	Chait - Sakhnovski
7	BUL	Denkova - Staviyski
8	GER	Winkler - Lohse
11	USA	Lang - Tchernyshev
23	USA	Handra - Sinek

Ice Hockey

Women's Hockey

Rank	Country
1	Canada
2	United States
3	Sweden
4	Finland
5	Russia
6	Germany
7	China
8	Kazakhstan

Men's Hockey

Rank	Country
1	Canada
2	United States
3	Russia
4	Belarus
5	Sweden
5	Germany
5	Finland
5	Czech Republic

Luge

Women's Singles

Rank	Country	Athlete	Score/Time
1	GER	Sylke Otto	2:52.464
2	GER	Barbara Niedernhuber	2:52.785
3	GER	Silke Kraushaar	2:52.865
4	AUT	Angelika Neuner	2:54.162
5	USA	Becky Wilczak	2:54.254
6	UKR	Lilia Ludan	2:54.499
7	AUT	Sonja Manzenreiter	2:54.537
8	USA	Ashley Hayden	2:54.658

Men's Singles

Rank	Country	Athlete	Score/Time
1	ITA	Armin Zoeggeler	2:57.941
2	GER	Georg Hackl	2:58.270
3	AUT	Markus Prock	2:58.283
4	USA	Adam Heidt	2:58.606
5	RUS	Albert Demtschenko	2:58.996
6	GER	Karsten Albert	2:59.046
7	GER	Denis Geppert	2:59.154
8	AUT	Markus Kleinheinz	2:59.211
17	USA	Tony Benshoof	3:00.102
26	USA	Nick Sullivan	3:01.566

Men's Doubles

Rank	Country	Athlete	Score/Time
1	GER	Leitner - Resch	1:26.082
2	USA	Grimmette - Martin	1:26.216
3	USA	Thorpe - Ives	1:26.220
4	GER	Skel - Woeller	1:26.375
5	CAN	Moffat - Pothier	1:26.501
6	AUT	Schiegl - Schiegl	1:26.518
7	ITA	Haselreider - Plankensteiner	1:26.616
8	AUT	Linger - Linger	1:26.684

Ski and Snowboard

Alpine Skiing

Women's Downhill

Rank	Country	Athlete	Score/Time
1	FRA	Carole Montillet	1:39.56
2	ITA	Isolde Kostner	1:40.01
3	AUT	Renate Goetschl	1:40.39
4	GER	Hilde Gerg	1:40.49
5	SUI	Corinne Rey Bellet	1:40.54
6	AUT	Selina Heregger	1:40.56
7	SUI	Sylviane Berthod	1:40.67
8	CAN	Melanie Turgeon	1:40.71
11	USA	Jonna Mendes	1:40.97
12	USA	Kirsten L Clark	1:41.03
16	USA	Picabo Street	1:41.17
—	USA	Caroline Lalive	DNF

Women's Combined

Rank	Country	Athlete	Score/Time
1	CRO	Janica Kostelic	2:43.28
2	AUT	Renate Goetschl	2:44.77
3	GER	Martina Ertl	2:45.16
4	SUI	Marlies Oester	2:46.61
5	AUT	Michaela Dorfmeister	2:46.85
6	USA	Lindsay Kildow	1:16.61
7	CAN	Genevieve Simard	1:18.26
8	SUI	Catherine Borghi	1:16.88
13	USA	Julia Mancuso	1:17.60
—	USA	Caroline Lalive	DNS

Women's Super Giant Slalom

Rank	Country	Athlete	Score/Time
1	ITA	Daniela Ceccarelli	1:13.59
2	CRO	Janica Kostelic	1:13.64
3	ITA	Karen Putzer	1:13.86
4	AUT	Alexandra Meissnitzer	1:13.95
5	GER	Hilde Gerg	1:13.99
6	AUT	Michaela Dorfmeister	1:14.08
7	FRA	Carole Montillet	1:14.28
8	AUT	Renate Goetschl	1:14.44
14	USA	Kirsten Clark	1:15.13
16	USA	Jonna Mendes	1:15.25
17	USA	Kathleen Monahan	1:15.59
—	USA	Caroline Lalive	DNF

2002 U.S. Olympic Team

Alpine Ski

Kirsten Clark **Lindsey Kildow** **Kristina Koznick** **Caroline Lalive** **Julia Mancuso**

Jonna Mendes **Katie Monahan** **Tasha Nelson** **Sarah Schleper** **Alex Shaffer** **Picabo Street**

 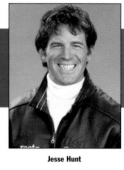    

Jake Fiala **Jesse Hunt** **Chip Knight** **Scott Macartney** **Bode Miller** **Casey Puckett**

Daron Rahlves **Tom Rothrock** **Erik Schlopy** **Dane Spencer** **Dale Stephens** **Marco Sullivan**

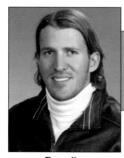     

Biathlon

Thomas Vonn **Andrea Nahrgang** **Kara Salmela** **Rachel Steer** **Kristina Sabasteanski**

∞ usa ✳ 2002

2002 U.S. Olympic Team

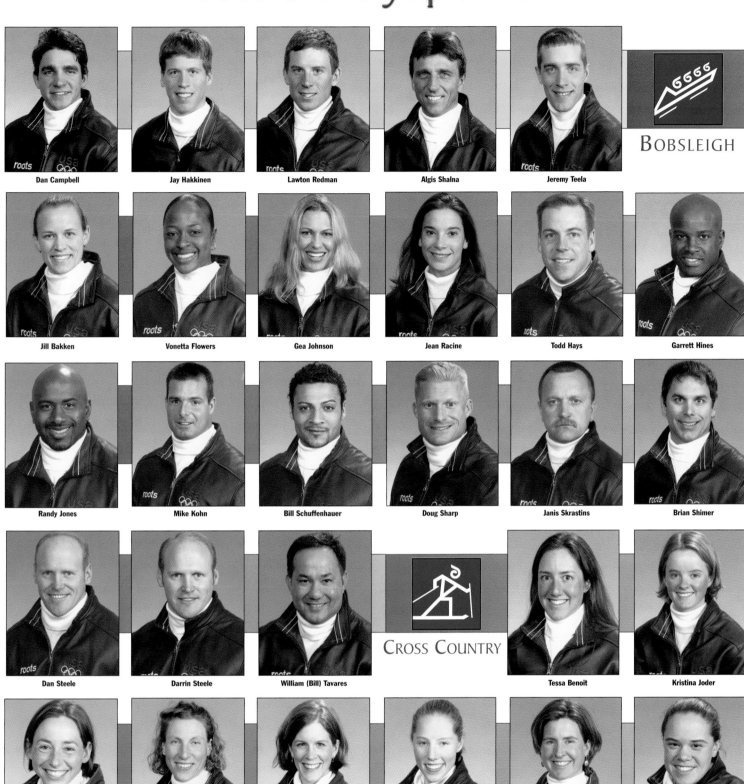

BOBSLEIGH

Dan Campbell   **Jay Hakkinen**   **Lawton Redman**   **Algis Shalna**   **Jeremy Teela**

Jill Bakken   **Vonetta Flowers**   **Gea Johnson**   **Jean Racine**   **Todd Hays**   **Garrett Hines**

Randy Jones   **Mike Kohn**   **Bill Schuffenhauer**   **Doug Sharp**   **Janis Skrastins**   **Brian Shimer**

CROSS COUNTRY

Dan Steele   **Darrin Steele**   **William (Bill) Tavares**   **Tessa Benoit**   **Kristina Joder**

Barb Jones   **Nina Kemppel**   **Aelin Peterson**   **Kikkan Randall**   **Wendy Wagner**   **Lindsey Weier**

usa*2002

189

2002 U.S. Olympic Team

John Bauer

Lars Flora

Kris Freeman

Andrew Johnson

Torin Koos

Christer Skog

Carl Swenson

Justin Wadsworth

Patrick Weaver

CURLING

Kari Erickson

Debbie McCormick

Stacey Liapis

Ann Swisshelm

Joni Cotten

Don Barcome, Jr.

Myles Brundidge

John Gordon

Mike Liapis

Mike Schneeberger

Raymond "Bud" Somerville

Tim Somerville

FIGURE SKATING

Sasha Cohen

Beata Handra

Tiffany Scott Hanson

Sarah Hughes

Kyoko Ina

Michelle Kwan

Naomi Lang

usa*2002

2002 U.S. Olympic Team

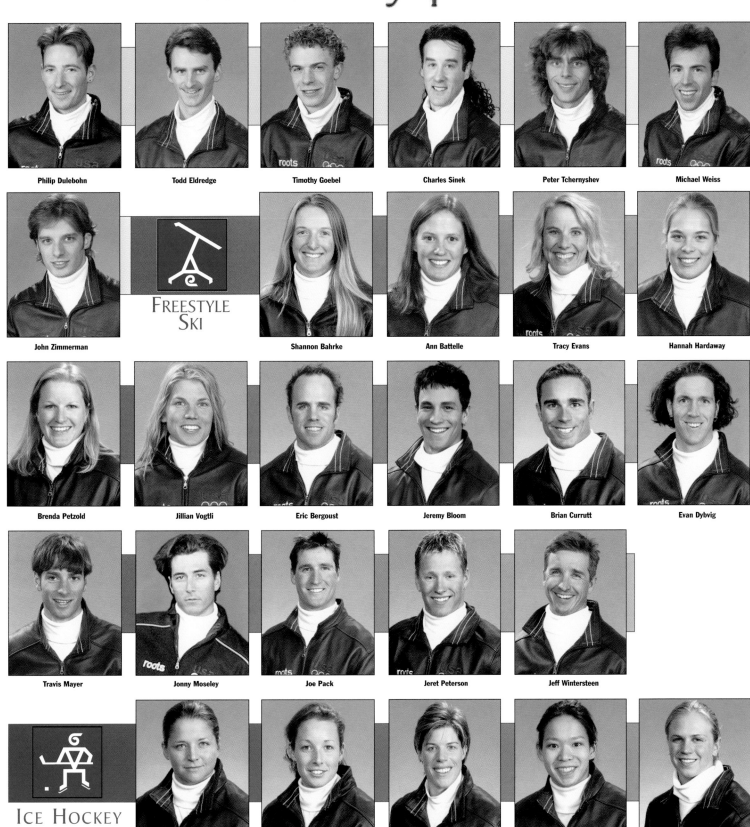

Philip Dulebohn

Todd Eldredge

Timothy Goebel

Charles Sinek

Peter Tchernyshev

Michael Weiss

John Zimmerman

FREESTYLE SKI

Shannon Bahrke

Ann Battelle

Tracy Evans

Hannah Hardaway

Brenda Petzold

Jillian Vogtli

Eric Bergoust

Jeremy Bloom

Brian Currutt

Evan Dybvig

Travis Mayer

Jonny Moseley

Joe Pack

Jeret Peterson

Jeff Wintersteen

ICE HOCKEY

Chris Bailey

Laurie Baker

Karyn Bye

Julie Chu

Natalie Darwitz

∞ usa*2002

191

2002 U.S. Olympic Team

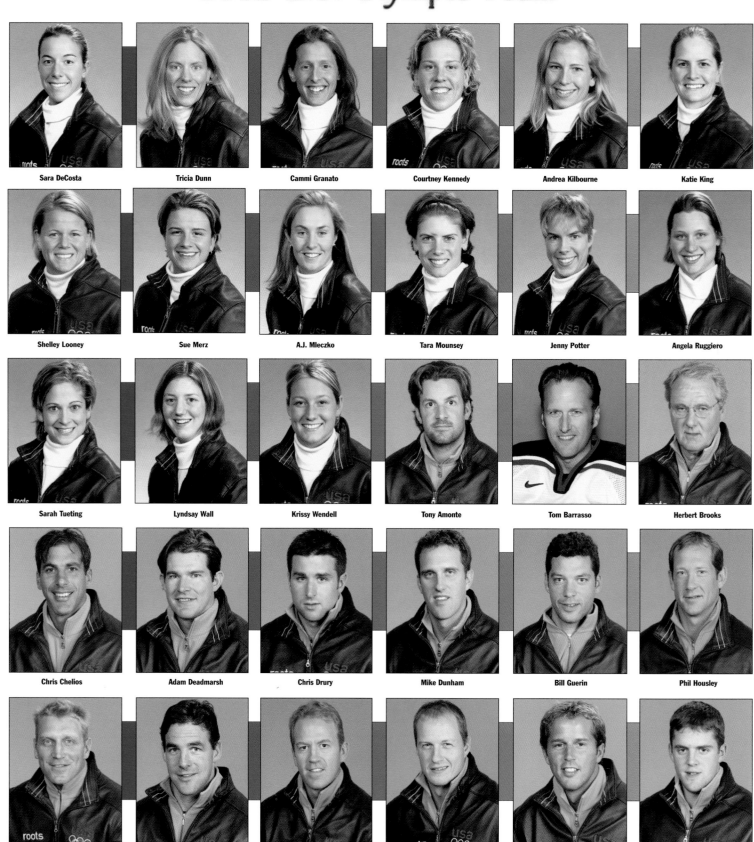

Sara DeCosta	Tricia Dunn	Cammi Granato	Courtney Kennedy	Andrea Kilbourne	Katie King
Shelley Looney	Sue Merz	A.J. Mleczko	Tara Mounsey	Jenny Potter	Angela Ruggiero
Sarah Tueting	Lyndsay Wall	Krissy Wendell	Tony Amonte	Tom Barrasso	Herbert Brooks
Chris Chelios	Adam Deadmarsh	Chris Drury	Mike Dunham	Bill Guerin	Phil Housley
Brett Hull	John LeClair	Brian Leetch	Aaron Miller	Mike Modano	Tom Poti

∞∞∞ usa∗2002

2002 U.S. Olympic Team

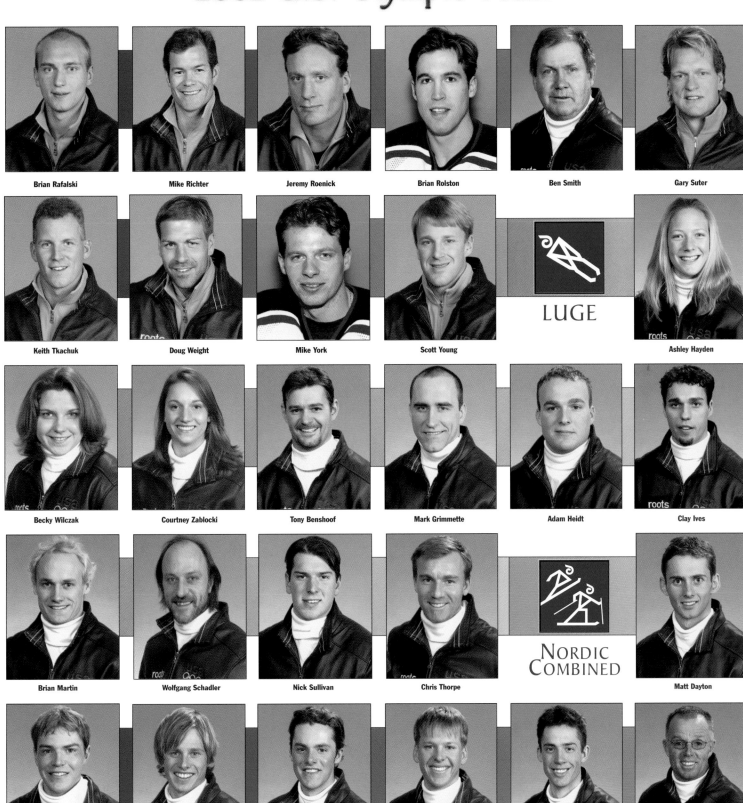

Brian Rafalski   Mike Richter   Jeremy Roenick   Brian Rolston   Ben Smith   Gary Suter

Keith Tkachuk   Doug Weight   Mike York   Scott Young   LUGE   Ashley Hayden

Becky Wilczak   Courtney Zablocki   Tony Benshoof   Mark Grimmette   Adam Heidt   Clay Ives

Brian Martin   Wolfgang Schadler   Nick Sullivan   Chris Thorpe   NORDIC COMBINED   Matt Dayton

Bill Demong   Kristoffer Erichsen   Jed Hinkley   Todd Lodwick   Johnny Spillane   Thomas Steitz

∞∞∞ usa*2002

193

2002 U.S. Olympic Team

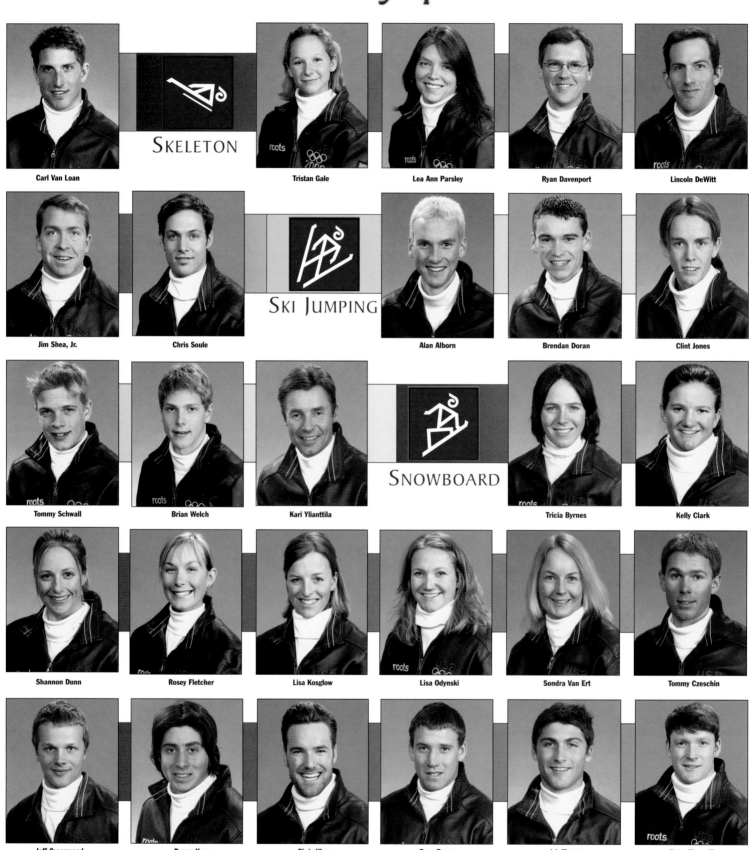

Carl Van Loan

SKELETON

Tristan Gale

Lea Ann Parsley

Ryan Davenport

Lincoln DeWitt

Jim Shea, Jr.

Chris Soule

SKI JUMPING

Alan Alborn

Brendan Doran

Clint Jones

Tommy Schwall

Brian Welch

Kari Ylianttila

SNOWBOARD

Tricia Byrnes

Kelly Clark

Shannon Dunn

Rosey Fletcher

Lisa Kosglow

Lisa Odynski

Sondra Van Ert

Tommy Czeschin

Jeff Greenwood

Danny Kass

Chris Klug

Ross Powers

J.J. Thomas

Peter Thorndike

usa*2002

2002 U.S. Olympic Team

SHORT TRACK SPEEDSKATING

Allison Baver Susan Ellis Julie Goskowicz Mary Griglak Caroline Hallisey

Amy Peterson Erin Porter Ron Biondo Shani Davis J.P. Kepka Apolo Anton Ohno

Rusty Smith Dan Weinstein **LONG TRACK SPEEDSKATING** Annie Driscoll Elli Ochowicz Catherine Raney

Jennifer Rodriguez Amy Sannes Becky Sundstrom Chris Witty K.C. Boutiette Kip Carpenter

Joey Cheek Michael Crowe Thomas Cushman Casey FitzRandolph Jason Hedstrand Derek Parra

∞∞∞ usa ∗ 2002

2002 U.S. Olympic Team

Nick Pearson

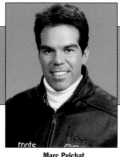
Marc Pelchat

Bartholome Schouten

J.P. Shilling

Jondon Trevena

⚬⚬⚬ usa ✳2002

(L-R) Kneeling: Tom Kelly, Kathleen Flynn, Jon Lundin, Juliann Fritz, Doug Haney, Cecil Bleiker, Chuck Menke. Standing: Bill Robertson, Ted Fragulius, Julie Urbansky, Nicole Jomantas, Laura Fawcett, Andy Fledderjohann, Lindsay DeWall, Dan Field, Irv Moss, Keslie Tomlinson, Kevin Neuendorf, Whitney Lovett, Nick Paulenich, Alexandra Cesteros, Rick Patzke, Suzie Paxton, Bob Dunlop, Matt Farrell, Carla O'Connell, Darryl Seibel, Bob Condron.
NOT PICTURED: Mike Moran, Nancy Chase, Jeff Howard, Lakesha Whitaker, Jim Constandt, Betsy McMillan, Cherylyn Underwood, Alan Ricks, Nate Hancock, Chris Condron, Erica Snaberger, Jay Howard, Heather Ahearn.

USA OLYMPIC DELEGATION MEDICAL STAFF

(L-R) Front Row: Bryon Craighead, Nick Metskas, Ray Barile, Dave Weinstein, Sara Delano, Robin Hunter, Maria Hutsick, Donna Flowers, John Pak, Jay Butcher, Ed Ryan. Back Row: John Hill, Kyle Wilkens, Dan Carr, Randy Vosters, Brad Stephens, Pat Karns, Mahlon Bradley, Chip Burke, Jim Ronai, Ed Merrens. Not Present: Terry Orr, Bill Sterett, Bryan Bomberg, Dave Joyner, Betsy Nadler, Dan Smith, Isaiah Tannaci, Jodi DeMaere.

USA OLYMPIC DELEGATION HEADQUARTERS STAFF

(L-R) First Row: Louise Bennett, Janet Venard, Jennifer Gabrius, Kim Bartkowski, Shelly Eller, Angela Scholze, Mary Bradley, Dave Bullock, Jeff Benz, Erin Kowalik, Mary Kay Parsons. Second Row: Liz Johnson, David Sellers, Terri Moreman, Becky Autry, Phyllis Phillips, Lee Stineman, Gary Johansen, Virginia Witte, Pat Rodgers, Keith Ferguson, Donna Raczynski. Third Row: Mike Wilson, Jim Ruby, George Hutchinson, Cindy Daybell, Dimitris Garglianos, Doug Karstens, Dave Clark, Jerry Searson, Patty Sturm, Robin Mann, Sean Pieri, Dianne Reynolds, Ron Karolick.
NOT PICTURED: Al Baeta, Tina Mendietta, Carol Williams,

USA OLYMPIC DELEGATION VILLAGE STAFF

(L-R) Dwight Bell, Gale Tanger, Jim McCarthy, Ed Devine, Abigail Tompkins, Cecil Bleiker, Francisco Campo, Rebecca Crawford, Chris Cole, Sherri Von Riesen, Gary Moy, Brendan Morris, Cindy Zielke, Randy Senger, Leslie Gamez, John Ruger, Heather Ross, Kirk Milburn.
NOT PICTURED: Felicia Zimmerman, Nathan Mills.

(L-R) Front row: Roger Condit, Wallace Sears and Darcy Steinfeld.
Back row: Whitney and Brittany DuBose, Chris Villines, Fran Henderson, Teri Hayt and Brad Sinclair.

Pachyderm Press.

George Mizzell

(L-R) Front row: Megan McLain and Keri Kahn.
Back row: Trey Mcclure, Shelly Marks, Michelle Joseph and Keith Dunn.
Unavailable for photo: Nathan Osmond

To Be An Olympian

Young Tristan Gale was limbering up at a young age. Tristan won the gold in women's skeleton.

photo courtesy of
U.S. Bobsled and Skeleton

Where do you go? Who do you call?

Where do you sign up?

"So you want to be a bobsledder Vonetta?"

"Well, Derek, being a speedskater takes practice. Do you know how to skate? "

"Hummm . . . you want to drive a skeleton, little Tristan? You'll have to wait until Halloween."

After watching the Olympic Winter Games and reading about the heroes on the ice and snow, millions of kids in living rooms and back yards around America are asking the same questions.

"How do I get involved?"

If a track coach in Alabama can be a gold medalist in bobsleigh, you can too. If an inline rollerskater from Florida can win two gold medals in his new sport of speedskating, you can too.

If a firefighter from Ohio can jump on a skeleton and blast head first down an icy chute . . . and love it . . . you can too.

You can be an Olympian. All it takes is a dream, some conviction . . . AND, most importantly, taking that first step. In this case, that first step is a phone call, or getting online and checking out a website.

The U.S. Olympic Committee is made up of a variety of organizations, including Olympic sports federations, or National Governing Bodies. Eight of these are Olympic Winter Sports. These federations would love to get those youngsters involved in their sports. But, first you have to ask.

For all those interested kids named Derek, Jim Jr., Michelle, Cammy, Picabo, Vonetta, Bode and whoever, take the first step. Get on a website and find out how to get involved. Make a phone call, go to the library.

One day you could be on that podium. Or you could just have fun in your neighborhood. Either way, you'll be a winner.

Previous page: Twelve-year-old Michelle Kwan placed sixth at the 1993 U.S. Figure Skating Nationals.

Contacts For More Information

U.S. Biathlon Association
29 Ethan Allen Ave.
Colchester, VT 05446
USBiathlon@aol.com

U.S. Bobsled and Skeleton
Federation
P.O. Box 828
Lake Placid, NY
   12946-0828
www.usabobsledandskeleton.org
518 344-1199

USA Curling
P.O. Box 866
Stevens Point, WI
   54481-0866
www.usacurl.org
715 344-1199

U.S. Figure Skating Association
20 First St.
Colorado Springs, CO
   80906-3697
www.usfsa.org
719 635-5200

USA Hockey
1775 Bob Johnson Dr.
Colorado Springs, CO
   80906
www.usahockey.org
719 576-8724

U.S. Luge Association
35 Church St.
Lake Placid, NY
   12946-1805
www.usaluge.org
518 523-2071

U.S. Ski and Snowboard
Association
P.O. Box 100
Park City, UT
   84060-0100
www.usskiteam.com
435 649-9090

U.S. Speedskating
P.O. Box 450639
Westlake, OH 44145
www.usspeedskating.org
440 899-0128 or
801 963-7125

U.S. Olympic Committee
One Olympic Plaza
Colorado Springs,
CO 80909
www.usolympicteam.com

Little Todd Hays, silver medalist in the four-man bobsleigh event.

photo courtesy of
U.S. Bobsled and Skeleton

205

IT'S NOT EVERY
IT'S
IT'S

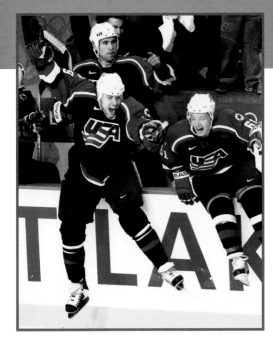

FOUR YEARS EVERY DAY.

IOC President Jacques Rogge
and Salt Lake City Mayor Rocky Anderson pass
the Olympic Flag to
Torino Mayor Sergio Chaimparino during
the Closing Ceremony of the
Salt Lake City Olympic Winter Games.

Elsa/Getty Images